TWENTIETH CENTURY
OF

MAJOR
BARBARA

A Collection of Critical Essays
Edited by
ROSE ZIMBARDO

Prentice-Hall, Inc.   A SPECTRUM BOOK   *Englewood Cliffs, N. J.*

Copyright © 1970 by Prentice-Hall, Inc., Englewood Cliffs, New Jersey. A SPEC-
TRUM BOOK. All rights reserved. No part of this book may be reproduced in
any form or by any means without permission in writing from the publisher.
C–13-545632-0; P–13-545624-X. *Library of Congress Catalog Card Number 72-104851.*
Printed in the United States of America.

Current printing (last number):
10 9 8 7 6 5 4 3 2 1

PRENTICE-HALL INTERNATIONAL, INC. (*London*)
PRENTICE-HALL OF AUSTRALIA, PTY. LTD. (*Sydney*)
PRENTICE-HALL OF CANADA, LTD. (*Toronto*)
PRENTICE-HALL OF INDIA PRIVATE LIMITED (*New Delhi*)
PRENTICE-HALL OF JAPAN, INC. (*Tokyo*)

Contents

Introduction

by Rose Zimbardo

I

The validity of the commonplace assertion that a piece of literature, in order to prove itself a work of art, must pass the test of time lies in the value it places upon historical distance; it is a comment not upon the work of art but upon the eye of the perceiver. Historical distance frees our sight from the distortions cast upon a work by the personality of its author and by our own experience, as the author's contemporaries, of the "reality," social and psychological, upon which he draws for the raw materials of his art. Distance allows us to see that any artist, however much he seems to himself or his times to be a social critic, a reformer, or a revolutionary, insofar as he is an artist must use the conditions of life as metaphors. In Suzanne Langer's words, "the moral content is thematic material, which, like everything that enters into a work of art, has to serve to make the primary illusion and articulate the pattern of 'felt life' the artist intends." [1] The work of art uses many and varied experiences to shape the form of a universal rhythm, the one fundamental experience of being human and of human being.

The phenomenon of distancing from a work of art to the point where we can recognize that it is a form of "felt life" is particularly relevant to *Major Barbara*, for it is only in the most recent present that the play has come to be so considered. Responding to the critics of his day, who accused him of not writing plays, Shaw called *Major Barbara*, not the exhibition of comic form that it is, not even a play, but "a discussion in three acts." Misreading Shaw's irony, or responding to the man himself as political activitist, critics from the first appearance of the play to the present have been misled into entering the "discussion." They have, consequently, trained their eyes upon the issues that a Shaw play raises, rather than upon the form, the pattern, the art that those metaphors shape. *Major Barbara* has

---

[1] "The Comic Rhythm," *Form and Feeling* (New York, 1953), p. 236.

been variously argued with. Like the rest of the Shaw canon, it has
been used to indict its author as "a good man fallen among Fabians," [2]
or an illogical thinker, or to praise him as a "rationalist," who "was
no poet, but . . . was a dramatist." [3] We have been led to consider
questions like how Shaw, a socialist, could make the character Andrew
Undershaft so attractive, instead of questions more relevant to Shaw's
art—for example, what function has the metaphor represented in
Andrew Undershaft in shaping the design of this play? Shaw himself warned us away from rationalistic literalness. He ends his Preface to *Major Barbara* with a guideline that would steer us clear of
historically bound, realistic half-truths to higher ground, to truth of
imagination.

> This play of mine, Major Barbara, is, I hope, both true and inspired;
> but whoever says it all happened and that faith in it and understanding
> of it consist in believing that it is a record of an actual occurrence, is,
> to speak according to Scripture, a fool and a liar, and is hereby solemnly
> denounced as such by me, the author, to all posterity.[4]

The revaluation of *Major Barbara,* for which we needed to be
freed by distance, has begun. The excerpt in this volume from
Martin Meisel's *Shaw and the Nineteenth Century Theater,* by show-
ing us that Shaw was not creating a new drama, but was merely forg-
ing new dramatic conventions out of old, can help us to recognize
the difference between the thematic form of the play and the devices
that shape that form. Joseph Frank's article, a pioneering view in
1956,[5] compares *Major Barbara* to *The Divine Comedy,* a poem
that in its time might well have been mistaken for a moral discussion.
The excerpt from Fred Mayne's *The Wit and Satire of Bernard Shaw*
is perhaps the best evidence of how far the critic of Shaw has been
liberated. Not only does Mayne have no need to enter into the discussion that takes place between Shaw's characters; he can view it
with a detachment so complete as to enable us to recognize it as
dramatic style, artistic structuring. Margery Morgan's article, written
this year, makes no apology for approaching the play as symbolic
form but freely explores the intricacy of its thematic design. I have
chosen these articles in the hope of providing as many angles as
possible for viewing a comedy that I consider to be one of the great
incarnations of comic form.

[2] Alick West, "A Good Man Fallen Among Fabians," *George Bernard Shaw*
(New York, 1950).

[3] Bruce R. Park, "A Mote in the Critic's Eye: Bernard Shaw and Comedy," *Texas
Studies,* XXXVII (1958), 195.

[4] Shaw, "Preface to Major Barbara," *Complete Plays and Prefaces,* I (New York:
Dodd, Mead, 1962), 339. All references to the play are to this edition.

[5] As recently as 1956 Frank had to indicate that he meant his comparison to be
"neither facetious nor hyperbolic."

II

Comedy abstracts, and reincarnates for our perception, the motion and rhythm of living.[6]

Major Barbara is not only a great comedy, but, like other Shaw plays, though more successfully, I think, than any other, it is a comedy about comedy. It is at once an assertion that the whole truth of being and existence is comic and a celebration of that truth. It has been said of Shaw that "he is not simply dissatisfied with certain human activities; he seems to be in rebellion against the very nature of human existence . . . [filled with] a kind of Swiftian digust at the human body and its functions." [7] Yet Shaw described himself as a "skilled voluptuary." Despite his employment of satire and irony as shaping devices, Shaw's vision is not the vision of a satirist. For him the truth is not that man is fallen from perfection, a slug forever doomed to crawl in mud, but that man is not yet perfect. Shaw uses irony and satire to blast away at the limitations that fear, ignorance, oppression, or self-delusion create for us. Breaking through limits is for Shaw the use as well as the joy of art. He once said that "the effect the artist produces in others is that of unlimitedness, and it is this great mystery and infinitude which attracts us all to art at first. . . ." [8] Comedy, in his words "is nothing less than the destruction of old-established morals." [9] Comedy's destructive power does not arise, however, from dissatisfaction with human imperfection, as satire's does; it is rather a joyous bursting through inhibiting and inadequate boundaries; it is the growing power of that which is alive. The function of art for Shaw was not just *utile,* to teach, but also *dulce,* to give joy, to enlarge the capacity for joy, to embody joy, which is to give form to the excitement of living itself. Shaw, following Schopenhauer and Nietzsche, believed that Being, the force that drives man's life and the life of the universe, is will, desire, passion.

Taking it, then, as established that life is a curse to us unless it operates as pleasurable activity, and that as it becomes more intense with the upward evolution of the race it requires a degree of pleasure which cannot be extracted from the alimentary, predatory and amatory instincts without ruinous perversion of them; seeing also, that the alternative

---

[6] Langer, *Form and Feeling,* p. 345.
[7] Robert Brustein, "Bernard Shaw: The Face Behind the Mask," p. 100.
[8] Shaw, *Platform and Pulpit,* ed. Dan H. Lawrence (New York, 1961), p. 45.
[9] Shaw, *Our Theatres in the Nineties,* III (London, 1948), p. 87.

of 'high thinking' is impossible until it is started by 'high feeling' to
which we can only come through the education of the senses—are we
to deliberately reverse our own Puritan traditions and aim at being a
nation of skilled voluptuaries? Certainly![10]

Shaw wrote comedies because comedy articulates the joy of being.
Major Barbara is an enactment of the great comic theme. The
germ of that theme is presented in the lines from Euripides that
Cusins quotes for Undershaft.

> . . . men in their millions float and flow
> And seethe with a million hopes as leaven;
> And they win their will; or they miss their will . . .
> But whoe'er can know . . .
> That to live is happy, has found his heaven.
>
> Is it so hard a thing to see
> That the spirit of God—whate'er it be,
> The law that abides and changes not, ages long
> The Eternal and Nature-born; these things be strong. (p. 386)

This is the thematic truth of *Major Barbara* and of all comedy:
Being is the highest good. The energy and immortality, not of the
individual life, but of life itself is heaven.

Nevertheless, we cannot overlook the destructive aspect of comedy.
Comedy celebrates endless being, an immense vitality that breaks
through and discards all outworn structures; if the pattern of comedy
is to work itself out, something must be broken. Therefore all comedy
contains within it the potentiality for tragedy. If we resist the excitement and rush of the comic rhythm and allow ourselves instead to
sympathize with the limited structured life that must be overthrown
by it—if we shed tears for Shylock, or experience more than a twinge
of anxiety for the chained and penned Malvolio—we are in danger
of tipping the balance and replacing the comic with the tragic experience. Shaw "insisted" to Henderson "that 'Major Barbara' might
easily have been transformed into a tragedy," [11] for this play has the
form of comedy yet incorporates the assertion that is made by tragedy.
It allows the expression of tragic truth within a comic design.

What then is the comic design? What is that "reincarnation of
the rhythm of living" that we perceive when we watch comedy? At
the risk of grave oversimplification, I think that we can say that the

---

[10] Shaw, "The Religion of the Pianoforte," *How to Become a Musical Critic*,
ed. Dan Lawrence (London, 1960), pp. 224–25.

[11] Shaw, in Archibald Henderson, *G. B. S.: Man of the Century* (New York, 1956),
p. 628.

shape we watch when we watch a comedy is a cycle in motion. What we see in comedy is the truth that the wealth and energy of being are inexhaustible, and the further truth that man, though in his pretentiousness always convincing himself that he is the master of his being, is really, rather, its servant. For these reasons most comedies are about love. In the simplest rendition of the comic formula a young couple is prevented by one of a thousand reasons from consummating their love (often the pretension of one of them to be above desire). They destroy the obstacles to their desire and come together, and the story ends with a communal feast and a wedding that promises a new generation that will, in its turn, desire, triumph, and so on. The truth even in so simplified a scheme is that individuating structures are obstacles to life. The impulse to apartness is broken, individuals are broken (often to be renewed), but mankind goes on forever because, fortunately, men are not the rational governors of their destiny, but its passionate servants.

The tragic truth is the other face of the human coin. It asserts that singular, individuated man is the highest good in the world. It proclaims that man, though doomed by the laws of his destiny to fall, is not a mindless animal driven by desire, but halfway angelic. In *Major Barbara* Shaw enlarges the comic circle to proportions that will accommodate the tragic truth. Whereas the lines from Euripides quoted above crystallize the comic truth that being is the highest good, the lines that follow ask tragedy's question:

> What else is Wisdom? What of man's endeavor
> Or God's high grace so lovely and so great?
> To stand from fear set free? to breathe and wait?
> To hold a hand uplifted over Fate?

Shaw answers the question by rounding out tragedy's arc. Man's will, individual man's energy, embodying and even enlarging life's energy, is the tragic assertion made whole and fitted to a conception of being larger than individual human being. Being, sheer livingness, is heaven, but the greater the energy of individual human being, the higher and truer the heaven.

Shaw's views on Creative Evolution are sometimes thought to be mere pseudoscientific claptrap, irrelevant to the understanding of his plays, but condescending to Shaw is always dangerous and in this case could blind us to an interesting theory of comedy. Creative Evolution is a theory of comedy, admittedly often awkwardly or extravagantly expressed, that applies not only to Shaw's comedies but to other great comedy as well. (It illuminates, for example, the late comedies of Shakespeare.) William Irvine provides an economical summary of Shaw's central idea.

Life began when the Life Force entered into matter and guided the
molecules into organic form. The Life Force is mind plus upward-striv-
ing will. In plants and animals it is relatively unconscious, manifesting
itself presumably through tropism and instinct; in man it is highly self-
conscious, manifesting itself through reason as well as instinct and
through an inward mystical sense to be cultivated by contemplation.
Man is its contrivance for building up intelligence, and woman its
contrivance for passing on such intelligence to the next generation,
for as a Lamarkian Shaw believes in the inheritance of acquired characteristics. Essentially Shaw's religion of the Life Force is an effort to
enlist the religious sense of mankind in the service of evolutionary
progress.[12]

III

The thematic form of *Major Barbara* is a cycle, which pushes
a new generation, a new divine couple, forward to replace the old.
Within this comic design is an upward expansion that enlarges the
dimension of the comic circle. The upward movement is effected in
the education of Barbara and Cusins, their growth to fullest human
capacity, that is, to becoming the wielders of power over life and death.
But though the comic design is enlarged, it is not replaced. The
structure of the play is not linear—a movement upward to greater
and greater understanding (the tragic movement)—but cyclical:
Barbara and Cusins replace Lady Britomart and Undershaft as the
new generators of that power which is Being. Just as the energy of
the Salvation Army "picks a waster out of the public house and makes
a man of him . . . finds a worm wriggling in a back kitchen and
lo! a woman" (p. 385), so the greater energy of the salvation of being
(which Shaw calls the Life Force), using as its medium their own
superior wills, creates a superman, Cusins, and a superwoman,
Barbara, to replace the strong man and woman that Undershaft and
Lady Britomart have been, for the purpose of carrying on and en-
riching the business of life. As often happens in comedy, the central
configuration in the play is sexual, not social or economic. Although
we are obliged by the necessity imposed by dramatic form to consider
the characters as people, if we do not look beyond the issues that
engage them to the movements that they shape, we are apt to miss
seeing that they are also symbolic principles, gods engaged in the
enactment of the cosmological dance of life that the play figures.
In the simplest manifestations of comic form it is usually the
older generation, petrified in their attitudes towards life and therefore no longer useful to it, who must be overthrown by the vigor of

[12] *The Universe of George Bernard Shaw* (New York, 1949), p. 242.

a new generation. Shaw, however, widens the scope of comedy; he not only allows us to see the comic movement from the viewpoint of a younger generation growing to occupy and enlarge the positions no longer adequately filled by their elders, but he also permits us a backward viewpoint by providing us an older generation who, still servants of life, generously hand over wealth and energy to their successors. This renders the comic pattern more complex, for the obstacles to life that must be overcome are not stock figures. They are rather psychological obstacles within the younger generation themselves. The barriers that must be broken by the push to full energy are inadequate self-conceptions held by Barbara and Cusins. Barbara thinks she has come to the fullest expression of her spirit in the Salvation Army; Cusins has been collecting religions, none of which quite fits his needs. The boundaries they must overcome are within them; the older generation, to whatever extent they can, serve as the younger generation's guides to wisdom. This widening of comic scope is reminiscent of Shakespeare's later comedies, most particularly of *All's Well That Ends Well*, a play that Shaw especially admired.

Because *Major Barbara* is a play that recognizes the validity of the tragic arc as the shape of individual life and subsumes that arc within the circular design of comedy, it is much concerned with inheritance. Undershaft and Lady Britomart are a wilting crescent, but they are concerned to hand on to a younger generation the power that they have wielded in their time. Undershaft freely admits that he is "getting on in years" and that Lazarus (waiting for resurrection?) "has insisted that the successor must be settled on one way or the other." "Father Colossus," whose love for his daughter is, as Cusins remarks, "the most dangerous of all infatuations," wants to win her so that she can propagate "the Undershaft inheritance," the inheritance of "the command of life and command of death." He must break the Salvation Army's hold upon her in order to break a delusory image that she has of herself. He breaks that image to prepare for the release of her true fire, to make her ready to receive his gift. He says, "I shall hand on my torch to my daughter."

Although much, overmuch, has been made of Undershaft, the importance of Lady Britomart has been grossly underestimated. Critics have seized upon Shaw's stage direction that Lady Britomart conceives the universe "as though it were a large house in Wilton Crescent" and have dismissed her as a caricature of the upper-class overbearing female without giving full weight to the rest of Shaw's description. He says that she is "well-dressed and yet careless of her dress, well-bred and quite reckless of her breeding, well-mannered and yet appallingly outspoken . . . amiable and yet peremptory, arbitrary

and high-tempered to the last bearable degree." There is a magnifi-
cent freedom and energy in Lady Britomart. Shaw is careful to describe her limitations (which, interestingly enough, she has had imposed upon her by "being treated as a naughty child until she grew
up into a scolding mother") but he is also careful to tell us of the
vitality with which she operates within those limitations. Though she
conceives the universe narrowly, she has "plenty of practical ability
and worldly experience" that enable her to "handle her corner of it
very effectively." The critics have also underestimated the significance
of Shaw's insistence to the actors that "the clue to much of Barbara
is that she is her mother's daughter." [13] Consequently, they have been
shocked that the play ends not with Barbara still enraptured, but
rather with Barbara and the sister from whom she has seemed so different clustering around and teasing their mother as Barbara nags:
"I want a house in the village to live in with Dolly. (Dragging at the
skirt.) Come and tell me which one to take." We cannot be shocked
when we remember that Shaw is writing a comedy and that comedy
rests on the assumption that the good of this world—the stuff and
matter of it—is a very great good.

The inheritance that Barbara and Cusins, the new divine couple,
receive is not just the torch of Undershaft's explosive fire, but also
flesh and blood, the gift of the woman, Lady Britomart, which is the
only material in which divine energy can express itself. Lady Britomart, the female principle, is the agent of material being, the vehicle
by which matter—as necessary to the Life Force as energy—has been
transmitted. She arranges marriages and provides that the money be
found to maintain them; she feeds and houses the family, straightens
and bullies it, and insists upon its endless continuity. The assertion
that her name is newspeak for "British Market"—the old order that
must be overthrown—is, I think, merely one angle (that of social
criticism) from which to view her position in the play. When we think
of the play as symbolic form, we are drawn naturally to make the
associations with Lady Britomart's name that are made by Nethercot:
it "has perhaps a double ancestry, for Britomart was Spenser's female
knight of chastity, and Britomartis was a Cretan deity, presiding over
hunting, fishing and the fruits of the earth." [14] There is no contradiction in the two associations, for Spenser's Britomart is the knight
of *married* chastity, the mother-to-be whose quest is to seek her husband that the race may be born. (Moreover, the association with female knighthood is particularly interesting when we remember that
Undershaft always refers to himself as an armorer.) Lady Britomart

[13] Archibald Henderson, *Bernard Shaw: Playboy and Prophet* (New York, 1932),
p. 808.
[14] Arthur Nethercot, *Men and Supermen* (Cambridge, 1954), p. 295.

treats all men as children because all men *are*, symbolically speaking, her children; her job as female servant of the life force has been to bring physical existence into being, to nourish and sustain it, and to insure its propagation. A large part of Barbara's education consists in her coming to accept her mother's materialistic wisdom. She has tried to mother, to nourish the growth of, men's souls without recognizing the importance of the bodies in which those souls must live. Her resemblance in manner to Lady Britomart as she bullies Bill in the Salvation Army shelter is clear, but it is the imitative gesturing of a child playing at being a mother. In the Salvation Army Barbara is "dressing up" as a woman. It is not until she comes to Perivale St. Andrew's that she has grown large enough to accept and enlarge upon her mother's wisdom.

> After all my dear old mother has more sense than any of you. I felt like her when I saw this place—felt that I must have it—that never, never, never could I let it go; only she thought it was the houses and the kitchen ranges and the linen and china, when it was really all the human souls to be saved. (p. 444)

The duality of human nature is what Shaw's comedy, and all great comedy, celebrates. Human souls, however noble and elevated, inhabit human bodies. Lady Britomart can be spirited, can be "careless" of her possessions and her breeding, because she respects the functional value of material good.

Major Barbara is, however, both major and Barbara; the young receive a dual inheritance, from the mother and also from the father. As Lady Britomart is material good, Undershaft is the good of will—the shaft "that through the green fuse drives the flower," or, if we are to use Shaw's terminology, the force that "entered into matter and guided the molecules into organic form" giving it, so to speak, armor. As Lady Britomart is the mother of all men, Undershaft is the principle of energy in all men. To keep his faith as an armorer he must give power to any man strong enough to "pay the price" for it, "without respect to persons or principles, to aristocrat and republican, to Nihilist and Tsar, to Capitalist and Socialist . . . to black man, white man, and yellow man, to all sorts and conditions, all nationalities and faiths, all causes and crimes." (p. 430) Will, energy, the power that drives life, is not morally, or in any way, differentiable. The great force that Undershaft serves is the power of being itself.

But what is that strength required to "pay the price"? It is in answering this question that Shaw gives full value to tragic truth while yet accommodating it to a comic rhythm. Undershaft is heroic, individuated man. His destiny is to widen as fully as he can, by the strength of his own will, the dimensions of being, and then to fall before the coming of his successor. His heir must be another individuated being, who, like him, "has no relations . . . who would be out of the running if he were not a strong man." Will, the power that moves matter, that drives the process of successive generation and Creative Evolution, although it enlivens matter, cannot be entrapped by it. No Undershaft can pass his power on to his natural son, as his wife, serving material continuity, must insist that he do; he must rather find a successor as free as he is (or freer with each succeeding generation) from the claims of blood. In order for will to thrive from generation to generation it must strive to free itself in each generation from the claims of matter. The potentiality for tragic irony in this pattern is obvious. Undershaft is modelled upon the Nietzschean conception of Dionysus. (He is specifically referred to as Dionysus several times in the play.) He is the tragic god, who must come to the fullest expression of power, and must then fall before the god reborn, the next Andrew Undershaft. The energy of being, to which Undershaft's great will has given its fullest expression in his generation, is the very power that must throw him over for his successor. However, in this play the tragic pattern takes place in the lap of comedy.

Energy with matter, male with female, individual will as the vehicle for, and the servant of, universal will: in these conjunctions Shaw creates the great comic theme—being is eternal—and fits to it the tragic theme—human greatness is the highest expression of being. It is in this respect that *Major Barbara* is a comedy about comedy, for the theory of creative evolution is a theory of comic rhythm. If Barbara and Cusins were merely replacements for Lady Britomart and Undershaft and the focus of the play were upon their coming together and removing the obstacles to inheritance, we would have a romantic, situational comedy, the simplest expression of the comic formula. This pattern is indeed present in the play; it is the convention of the sex comedy. Shaw enlarges this convention into comic theme. The pure sense of "felt life," "the motion and rhythm of living" that comedy articulates is for him not merely repetition, man following man in an endless succession of folly, but growth—man following man and, with each turning of the cycle, the pulse and rhythm of life strengthening. As Harold Fromm puts it ". . . Shaw regarded sex (and consequently comedy) as serious because it was the chief agent of the Life Force in the process which made the son intellectually and morally superior to his father." [15] In order to become the divine couple for their generation Barbara and Cusins must grow to be fully them-

---

[15] Harold Fromm, *Bernard Shaw and the Theatre of the Nineties* (Lawrence, Kansas, 1967), p. 62.

selves, and in doing so they will necessarily be superior to Lady Britomart and Undershaft. To become themselves they must break through all their illusions, all inadequate formulations of themselves. Their education is the play's means of taking the measure of man.

Barbara's vital energy must push through inadequate selves as a child must grow through the successive stages of childhood to come to its realization of manly or womanly power. We see her first in Wilton Crescent, the home provided for her by her parents. We must assume, from the discussion between Lady Britomart and Stephen that opens the play, that, like Stephen, Barbara knows nothing of the source of the money that supports the household. It is Lady Britomart, and not Barbara herself, who is arranging that Barbara's future shall be as materially comfortable as her past has been. In the first act, then, Barbara accepts, without recognizing, the "givens" of money and the freedom from concern for material well-being that money provides, power. She thinks that she has freed herself from material good and that she has therefore already liberated her spirit, but all that she has done is to "dress up" in the uniform of the Salvation Army. If she has decided, as a child might, to live on an allowance, that allowance, however small, is provided by her parents. Her most severe limitation at the beginning of the play, then, is that having no material needs, she makes the error of thinking that spiritual freedom rests upon the denial of material need. She is not sufficiently self-reflective to trace the material sources of her power. (It is significant, for example, that a great deal of the power that Barbara exercises over Bill Walker derives initially from her being an earl's granddaughter.) Nevertheless, despite her limitations, within the physical good that Barbara has inherited there operates a fiery spirit, which she has also inherited.

The centrally symbolic scene in Act I is the "blood and fire" religious service that Barbara conducts in the drawing room of Wilton Crescent. Barbara is right here in assuming that because the spirit of God is everywhere, a religious service can be conducted anywhere. She is wrong, however, in failing to recognize that her spirit, and therefore God's spirit, is enclosed here by the comfortable walls of her mother's house. Barbara sets herself apart from the other young people by virtue of her uniform and motto; she sees herself as already chosen by God. Lady Britomart's vision is limited in the opposite direction. In her eyes all the young people are equally her giggling irresponsible charges; she can see nothing more in Barbara's spirit than childish willfulness. Undershaft, on the other hand, who has given Barbara her spirit, will recognize it instantly. At this point in the play Barbara does not know herself sufficiently to realize that her freedom to be a spiritual being has been provided for her by Undershaft and Lady Britomart. She will learn that material nature must be satisfied, not denied, if its finitude is ever to be escaped.

Her second expression of vital power takes place in the Salvation Army "shelter." This has been her spirit's home, the place to which it fled from the confines of Wilton Crescent. But though the Salvation Army's shelter is deceptively larger than the shelter provided by her parents, it is, as Undershaft proves, no less a shelter from reality, and therefore no less inadequate as a defining form. As we have seen, Barbara unconsciously uses here a power not wholly derived from her own will but provided by her social position. The point that Shaw makes in this scene is that the body is always with us. Even without her social position, Barbara would take with her her inheritance of material well-being if only by virtue of being well-fed, robust, and jolly. Rather than ignore or deny material good, we must exploit it for the greatest amounts of energy it can provide. It is only then that we can refine upon the uses to which we put that energy.

More important, however, than Barbara's refusal to recognize the flesh as the source of human energy is her inability to see the boundary of illusion that she has imposed upon her spirit. In her image of herself she is still a child, watched over and protected by a heavenly Father. Looking back from Act III on her position in the Army, Barbara says,

> I stood on a rock I thought eternal; and without a word of warning it reeled and crumbled under me. I was safe with an infinite wisdom watching me, an army marching to Salvation with me; and in a moment at the stroke of your pen in a chequc book, I stood alone; and the heavens were empty. (p. 432)

Barbara has had to realize that the rock upon which human beings stand is not the rock envisioned by her imagination but the earth itself; that the spirit of God envisioned as a protective, overlooking eye is a self-limiting illusion, for the spirit of God is the spirit of life, which is in us, not outside us; and that the heavens *are* empty unless man's spirit mounts to fill them. Undershaft's pen is the sword of truth that rends the veil of her illusions. When, in Act III, she does come to these truths, she "goes right up to the skies." In tragedy when man's spirit mounts to the skies, it breaks against limits set upon it by some external, universal law (the gods, Fate, or destiny). In comedy, particularly Shavian comedy, man's spirit is the spirit of life itself and is eternal. Men break; man goes on forever.

The third "blood and fire" religious service in the play is the occasion for the final emergence of the force of being. It is held without Barbara, for she has been made to see that in the Salvation Army she has not been wielding spiritual power but has been at the child's game of playing at power within a system enclosed by Bodger and Undershaft. The centrally symbolic scene here, the scene that breaks Barbara and thereby prepares her to be the woman who will emerge at the end of the play, is the triumphal march to the docks. The Army here is transformed from Mrs. Baines' army, begging for bread, to an army triumphantly led by "Dionysus" Undershaft and Cusins, his successor. Undershaft is blowing "the Trumpet in Zion" that brought down the walls of Barbara's shelter. The music to which they march is "a wedding chorus from one of Donizetti's operas" that has been transformed by the Salvation Army to the march "Blood and Fire." This music is the governing metaphor for the action of the scene. "Blood and fire," emblematic throughout the play of the force of being, breaks individuated form to free the spirit within it. This marching music breaks Barbara's heart. But "blood and fire" is also another strain, a wedding march; within the very breaking is the promise of renewal and rebirth. In the burst of energy that the music sounds, two individuated figures are broken, the outmoded image of Barbara, who cries the words of the crucified Christ ("My God, why have you forsaken me?"), and the outworn image of the god of energy, Undershaft, who cries words symbolic of his reign, "my ducats and my daughter," the words of another gigantic figure whose "law" was proved by life and love to be too narrow. Undershaft in his time has drawn from material good the highest vitality of which he was capable. He falls to be replaced by Cusins, whose words in this scene, "money and gunpowder," foretell his own growth to "command of life and command of death." At this stage in her development Barbara conceives of the power negatively. She sees in the march only the triumph of "drunkenness and murder." She has not yet learned that divine energy is neutral and can only be directed by a human will strong enough to seize it and, by seizing it, to serve it.

The configuration of tragedy is present in this fall of the structured human figure, but it is not allowed to triumph over comic truth. In Act III Undershaft, looking back upon the scene with Barbara, tells her not to "make too much of [her] little tinpot tragedy." Cusins, his successor, cries out to the broken Barbara "What is a broken heart more or less here? Dionysus Undershaft has descended. I am possessed," and thereby proves himself worthy of succession. Comedy triumphs by insisting that a form too old, too rigid, or too small to contain life must be broken to be cast anew, for the wealth and energy of being are inexhaustible. Moreover, as man's body must grow to express the fullest vitality of which it is capable, and as his spirit must grow straining always against finitude, so must his imagination stretch to describe that which it strives to contemplate, the nature of being. As Undershaft, the spokesman of vital energy, puts it, "If your old religion broke down yesterday, get a newer and a better one for tomorrow."

At the end of the play Barbara, having come through "the valley of the shadow of death," can accept life. She has come to see that building and breaking are equally necessary activities of divine energy. As a woman she, of course, allies herself with the constructive movement of energy. But she is ready now to stand in proper, complementary relation to the new Undershaft, Cusins. She has come to womanhood in learning the value of the body as well as the spirit, in recognizing that the spirit of God can manifest itself only in living human bodies. She becomes the super-Britomart when she can say,

> Let God's work be done for its own sake; the work He had to create us to do because it cannot be done except by living men and women. When I die let Him be in my debt, not I in his; and let me forgive Him as becomes a woman of my rank. (p. 444)

We can assume that she too will handle her "corner" of the universe "very effectively."

As Barbara moves through widening definitions of herself, Cusins moves to an ever-increasing understanding of his own male energizing power. A man's problem goes beyond the woman's problem of learning to *do* most fully; he must also come to understand, to *know* the power that moves him and that he must come to move. Cusins begins with a quite personal view of will: "Whenever I feel that I must have something, I get it sooner or later." As we have seen, it is Shaw's view that "Higher thinking" and "Higher feeling" begin with personal desire. As Barbara's lively and robust nature is the given that sets her on the proper course to fulfillment, so Cusins' strong will and his unwillingness to settle for conventional or rigid definitions are the natural gifts that lead him toward truth, even when he cannot clearly see the truth. He does recognize that he is driven by will and he refuses to hamper the operation of his will with inadequate definitions of its nature. Shaw tells us that Cusins' desire to marry Barbara is impelled "by some instinct which is not merciful enough to blind him with the illusions of love." Moreover, being a "collector of religions" he is wise enough not "to wrangle about the name" of the unnameable. He does not, as Barbara does, envision God as a divine overseer. Rather, from the beginning of the play he is capable of seeing that a divine will drives the universe; it is, after all, he who quotes the lines from Euripides.

He must come by the end of the play to answer the question put in those lines: "But what of man's endeavor?" Interestingly, the very triumphal march that breaks Barbara's heart and prepares for the liberation of her spirit is Cusins' initiation rite. He is, as he says, first "possessed" and then intoxicated. He is careful to make it clear that it was not Undershaft who made him drunk: "No, he only provided the wine. I think it was Dionysus who made me drunk." Cusins has always recognized that the spirit of the universe is will, but he has not recognized his participation in that spirit. Undershaft has provided the means, but it is only by an act of his own will that Cusins can become Undershaft's successor. He must choose to join his will to the divine will. He must assume command of life and death, because it is only through the will of men and women that God's work can be done.

The instinct that drives him to want to marry Barbara is divine will operating constructively to bring forth new life. But that same will is also destructive of old, lifeless forms. In electing to become the new Undershaft Cusins accepts the truth of the totality of being. He will now put power into the hands of any man strong enough to pay the price for power, any man strong enough to direct it. When he has made the choice that he alone could make and that he had to make alone, standing free even of Barbara, Cusins comes to the full possession of manhood. Significantly, Barbara, now come to womanhood, announces that had Cusins not elected to be her father's successor, she would have married the man who had. They have come to understand the way in which each complements the other. For Barbara it is now not God, but her "Dolly boy" who has found her "place" and her "work" for her. As we saw in the quotation from Irvine above, "Man is [the world will's] contrivance for building up intelligence, and woman its contrivance for passing on such intelligence to the next generation."

The end of the play, the descent from those lyrical flights in which Barbara and Cusins discover themselves, recapitulates the great comic truth. Being renews itself with a man and a woman in a house in a village. Like a small stone thrown into a pool, that event, the smallest collision of energy with matter, sends widening rings of being to the furthest reaches of the cosmos.

PART ONE

Interpretations

Shaw and the Nineteenth Century Theater

by Martin Meisel

The Discussion Play is a genre in its own right, amenable to positive definition. It may be, however, that to make the claim is to fall into a trap for obsessive criticism; for there is no question but that Shaw used the term "Discussion" to flaunt his impatience with constricting academic definitions. The view of the academic purists is satirized in *Fanny's First Play* when Fanny speaks to the critic Trotter (a genial caricature, in academic uniform, of A. B. Walkley) about the avant-garde repertory-theater play:

> *Trotter (emphatically).* I think I know the sort of entertainments you mean. But please do not beg a vital question by calling them plays. . . .
> *Fanny.* The authors dont say they are.
> *Trotter (warmly).* I am aware that one author, who is, I blush to say, a personal friend of mine, resorts freely to the dastardly subterfuge of calling them conversations, discussions, and so forth, with the express object of evading criticism. But I'm not to be disarmed by such tricks. I say they are not plays. Dialogues, if you will. Exhibitions of character, perhaps: especially the character of the author. Fictions, possibly . . . But plays, no. I say NO. Not plays. (p. 261)

The initial reviews of *John Bull's Other Island* had found it particularly discursive, formless, and "not a play." [1] Shaw accordingly called

From Shaw and the Nineteenth Century Theater *by Martin Meisel (Princeton, N.J.: Princeton University Press, 1963), pp. 290–303, 32, 33. Reprinted by permission of Princeton University Press and Oxford University Press.*

[1] For example, "E. F. S.," in *The Sketch*, called *John Bull's Other Island* "Mr. Shaw's goodness-knows-what. . . . To me the play was vastly entertaining, despite its excessive length and total lack of form . . . of course, much of it is irrelevant . . . and of course, it was plotless" (9 Nov. 1904, p. 122). The reviewer in *The Illustrated London News* declared: "It is not a play . . . no, it is not a play, but something much more interesting—a series of loosely connected, almost disconnected scenes, in the progress of which the dramatist, through the mouths of his char-

his next major effort *Major Barbara, A Discussion in Three Acts*. Alone, *Major Barbara* would not have established a genre; but by the time Shaw dramatized Trotter's complaint in *Fanny's First Play*, he had added *Getting Married, A Conversation* (later called *A Disquisitory Play*) and *Misalliance, A Debate in One Sitting*. When these plays are taken together, it is evident that the Discussion Play is a distinct genre with defining characteristics and that it was a realization and culmination of tendencies evident in Shaw's earlier work, dating particularly from just after the period of the melodramas. *John Bull's Other Island* and the detachable third act of *Man and Superman* were discussion plays without the name. *Major Barbara* was a deliberate experiment in the potentialities of the genre. *Getting Married* and *Misalliance* were its mature fruits. *Heartbreak House*, as I shall try to show, was alchemically speaking its perfection and sublimation.

The joke in Shaw's substitution of the terms "discussion," "conversation," and "debate" for "drama," or "comedy," or "play" is that there was no joke. In his expansion of the early *Quintessence of Ibsenism* ("Completed to the Death of Ibsen" after *Misalliance* and before *Heartbreak House*), Shaw constructs a poetics of modern drama in which he offers "the discussion" as "a new technical factor in the art of popular stage-play making" which every considerable playwright has been using for a generation:

> Formerly you had in what was called a well made play an exposition in the first act, a situation in the second, and unravelling in the third. Now you have exposition, situation, and discussion; and the discussion is the test of the playwright. . . . The discussion conquered Europe in Ibsen's Doll's House; and now the serious playwright recognizes in the discussion not only the main test of his highest powers, but also the real centre of his play's interest. (*Quintessence,* p. 135)

Once introduced, the discussion did not remain a simple feature of an otherwise ordinary play. Shaw offers, as the primary technical novelty of the Ibsen and post-Ibsen plays, "the introduction of the discussion and its development until it so overspreads and interpenetrates the action that it finally assimilates it, making play and discussion practically identical" (*Quintessence,* p. 146). In Shaw's developmental view of Ibsen's innovation, the discussion in *A Doll's House* was only the beginning; the Discussion Play proper was, in effect, the end.

Shaw's view of the role of the discussion in his own work was similarly developmental. In a later "dialogue" constructed from his an-

acters, expresses his views on a multitude of topics connected with the distressful country and its problems and its various classes of people and its predominant partner" (125 [19 Nov. 1904], p. 719).

swers to a written questionnaire, Shaw speaks again of the birth of the Discussion Play at the end of *A Doll's House,* where Nora says, "We must sit down like two rational beings and discuss all this that has been happening between us":

> But the discussion, though at first it appears as a regularly placed feature at the end of the last act, and is initiated by the woman, as in *A Doll's House* and *Candida,* soon spreads itself over the whole play. Both authors and audiences realise more and more that the incidents and situations in a play are only pretences, and that what is interesting is the way we should feel and argue about them if they were real. . . . In *A Doll's House* and *Candida* you have action producing discussion; in *The Doctor's Dilemma* you have discussion producing action, and that action being finally discussed. In other plays you have discussion all over the shop. Sometimes the discussion interpenetrates the action from beginning to end. Sometimes, as in *Getting Married* and *Misalliance,* the whole play, though full of incident, is a discussion and nothing else.[2]

In its fully developed form, the Discussion Play was marked by the total subordination of incident to discussion, even though, as Shaw remarks, the given plays might be full of incident. As a matter of fact, *Getting Married* and *Misalliance* are remarkably crowded with incident because they have been freed so completely from that re-straining logic which required an "unravelling" of all the ingenious circumstances of the ingenious situation in the well-made play. In-stead, incident can now be used as point of departure, as illustration, or as emphatic resolution of some crisis of the argument. Action is governed by thought. Though the logic of dialectic is different from that of "construction," it is no less strenuous; but from the point of view of orthodox dramaturgy, there had been a great loosening of elements, giving that quality of crowded and extravagant improvisa-tion more generally found in Farce. . . .

The subordination of incident to dialectical exigencies is the funda-mental formula of the mature Discussion Play. On this foundation other qualities rest, and a descriptive definition of the genre must take into account the following technical characteristics: a central subject of discussion, as in the Platonic dialogues and Shaw's own prefaces, but a free resort to the entire intellectual universe of G.B.S.; a familiar center of reference in a genre associated with the subject of discussion, but a freely improvisatory handling of the basic conventions of that genre; a systematic use of representative social types in addition to representative figures embodying values and points of view. These common features are realized in *Major Barbara, Getting Married, Misalliance,* and *Heartbreak House.* They inhere in a full-fledged

[2] Archibald Henderson, "George Bernard Shaw Self-Revealed," *Fortnightly Review,* 125 (1926), 434–35.

genre, as characteristic of Shaw's "middle period" as Melodrama of
the early period and Extravaganza of the late.

Major Barbara

Major Barbara only partly suits Shaw's description of the full-
developed Discussion Play, for the centrality and seriousness of Barbara makes her story, her passion, dominate the other elements in
the first half of the play. Up to the point where she cries, "My God:
why hast thou forsaken me?" *Major Barbara* is not a full-fledged Discussion Play; but thereafter it is entirely so, even though Barbara
finds a second vocation, experiences a second spiritual upheaval sche-
matically equal to the first. In the last scenes, where incident is fully
subordinated to discussion, Shaw carefully takes the primary attention off Barbara's story. (In the early shelter scenes, Barbara's struggle
for her soul was direct. In the late arms-factory scenes, it is managed
through a surrogate, for Undershaft is apparently engaged in seducing,
not Barbara, but her affianced lover, Adolphus Cusins.) Nevertheless,
the schematized movement of *Major Barbara* culminates in, first, Barbara's conversion from Christianity, and, second, equally important,
her conversion to the Gospel of Andrew Undershaft. Her fall is only
the prelude to her redemption, so that we have, not a discussion tacked
on to an action, but an entire action treated first in one key, with an
interest in persons and events dominating discussion, then in another
key, with an interest in discussion dominating persons and events. It
is noteworthy that in the succeeding Discussion Plays there is no character as central as Barbara. Instead there is always the sense of a group
whose total interplay is valued for itself, rather than for the way it
affects any particular individual.

The central subject of discussion is religious and social morality,
and characters like Barbara, Lady Britomart, Stephen and Andrew
Undershaft, Peter Shirley and Bill Walker are spokesmen for moral
points of view. The genre principally invoked to supply a theatrical
frame of reference for the discussion is that best suited to the subject,
Melodrama. Shaw had already tried the usefulness of Melodrama to
present the temptations, perils, and spiritual discoveries of a Bun-
yanesque pilgrim. Like the Devil's Disciple and Captain Brassbound,
Major Barbara undergoes conversion and finds a true vocation, a
valid morality, or what amounts to the same thing for her, a valid
religion.

Major Barbara shows two of the observable common characteristics
of the Discussion Play in possessing a central subject of discussion
(Christian and un-Christian moralities) and a familiar genre appro-

priate to the subject as a center of theatrical reference. It shows a third characteristic in making use of representative social types in addition to characters speaking for values and moral points of view. Lady Britomart, in addition to being "the incarnation of morality," represents an unreconstructed aristocracy; Undershaft, the foundling, represents an essentially classless plutocracy. That Barbara is her aristocratic mother's as well as her foundling father's daughter when she marries the philosopher is as important to the philosophical-political resolution of the play as Plato's suggestion, "that society cannot be saved until either the Professors of Greek take to making gunpowder, or else the makers of gunpowder become Professors of Greek" (*Barbara*, p. 439). Peter Shirley and Snobby Price represent, between them, the working class. Peter Shirley is conscientious, profitable (to his employers), and honest, "and what av I got by it?" (p. 390). Snobby Price, who has none of these virtues, describes himself as "an intelligent workin man. . . . In a proper state of society I am sober, industrious and honest: in Rome, so to speak, I do as the Romans do" (p. 367). He speaks not for himself only but for a social contingent. In the Discussion Plays which followed *Major Barbara*, this technique was to become increasingly important until *Heartbreak House*, in which there is a fusion of the subject of discussion and these representative social types.

In the course of composition, Shaw summarized the first part of *Major Barbara* as follows:

> [Barbara] is a religious young pusson, who has been a wonderful success in the Salvation Army, making converts in all directions, and, as to violent and brutal roughs who beat women on the stage in the most melodramatic manner, she stands them on their heads as if they were naughty children. . . . Her father, who is fond of her (he meets her for the first time practically in the first act) has a most terribly wicked religion of his own, believing only in money and gunpowder; and he finally gets her turned out of the Army as an enemy of religion in a very subtle and very simple way.[3]

The melodramatic associations of *Major Barbara* cluster around the relationship between Barbara and her father, though there are other reminiscences of Melodrama which contribute to the generic reference, such as the stagey asides that pass between Cusins and Undershaft in the presence of Barbara, the question of the inheritance, and the familiar motif of the foundling heir.[4] But fundamental to the

[3] Eleanor Robson Belmont, *The Fabric of Memory* (New York, 1957), p. 39. (Letter dated 4 July 1905.)

[4] Shaw inverts the last device, for Cusins is obliged to prove he is a foundling before he can qualify as the true heir. (Stephen, the legitimate son, is kept out of the inheritance, on principle.) Examples of straightforward use of the foundling heir

melodramatic reference of the play is the conventional relationship between the passionate, designing "heavy" [5] and the fair, spiritual heroine who is protected by the aureole of her innocence as Barbara feels she is protected by her uniform.

*   *   *

[The following paragraphs are taken from pp. 32–33 of the text.]
Undershaft in *Major Barbara* is the most notable embodiment in Shaw's drama of ideas of the melodramatic Heavy as vital genius.
. . . Both Undershaft and Mendoza, another Shavian leader of great natural energy and passion, have the Heavy's mesmeric force; but Mendoza, like Brassbound, is factored into impotence by his romanticism, while Undershaft is multiplied into irresistible force by his visionary sense of reality. To Louis Calvert (who played a number of his personages in the heavy line) Shaw wrote:

> I am getting on with the new play, scrap by scrap, and the part of the millionaire cannon founder is becoming more and more formidable. Broadbent and [K]eegan rolled into one, with Mephistopheles thrown in: that is what it is like. . . . Undershaft is diabolically subtle, gentle, self-possessed, powerful, stupendous, as well as amusing and interesting. . . . That penny-plain and twopence-colored pirate Brassbound will be beneath your notice then.

Shaw dictated to Calvert that Undershaft, like Bohun, should absolutely take charge of the end of the play. "Undershaft must go over everybody like Niagara from that moment. . . . His energy must be proof against everybody and everything."

*   *   *

Like Jacob M'Closky in Boucicault's *Octoroon,* like the tormented,

---

are in Edward Fitzball's *Daughter of the Regiment* (1843), where Madelaine has been found on the battlefield of Marengo, and is identified long after as the niece of a Marchioness; in T. J. Lynch's *Rose of Ettrick Vale* (1829; based on Scott), where Albert, a foundling, is really the heir of the Leonards, and recovers his inheritance from the usurping Red Ronald; and in Tom Taylor's *The Serf* (1865), where Ivan is thought to be, at best, the illegitimate son of the old Count and the hated serf of the new, and turns out to be the legitimate son and true heir after all. J. R. Planché, in *The Brigand, A Romantic Drama in Two Acts* (1829), anticipates with romantic seriousness Gilbert's burlesque of the privileges of orphanhood in *The Pirates of Penzance.* In *The Brigand,* Albert, who has been captured, requests to be let go to fetch his own ransom: "Let the belief in your generosity which has inspired so novel a proposition, be the pledge of the sincerity with which it is made. That, and his oath, are all a poor foundling has to offer. (MASSARONI, *affected, drops gun. Brigands advance a little, listening.*) MAS. (*starting.*) A foundling? abandoned by your parents? (*A pause.*) Enough, I will trust you . . ." (*French S. D.*, p. 14).
   [5] Shaw spoke of the role as "the enormously difficult and heavy part of Barbara's father" (Belmont, *Fabric of Memory*, p. 49).

passionate Meadows in Reade's *It's Never Too Late To Mend,* like the lawyer-agent Coyle in Tom Taylor's *Our American Cousin,* like the gentlemanly Loftus in Falconer's *Eileen Oge,* Undershaft plans first to beggar his victim, by cutting her off from existing supports, and then to get her into his power. M'Closky ruins the Peytons, Zoe's protectors, and buys her as a slave in the forced sale of the plantation; Loftus has Eileen's lover transported and wins her through his power to ruin or save her father. And like these heavy lawyers and rent-agents of Melodrama whose dark passions disqualify them for straightforward wooing, Undershaft realizes he must capture Barbara by indirection. In the scene in which he plots her downfall, he tells Cusins, Barbara's lover, "My friend: I never ask for what I can buy."

> Cusins (*in a white fury*). Do I understand you to imply that you can buy Barbara?
> Undershaft. No; but I can buy the Salvation Army. (p. 389)

In this preliminary project he is, from Barbara's point of view, successful. By paying to the Salvation Army a few thousand pounds, and emphasizing that these are the devil's profits in misery, he cuts Barbara off from her external resources. In effect he robs and beggars her in order to offer her the sinister comforts of his home.[6]

Having bought away the Army in the first part of the play, Undershaft buys away Cusins in the last. Having turned Barbara out of her old religion, he tempts her with the splendors and comforts of his new one. And having seen Undershaft's heavenly city, Barbara, like her mother, "felt I must have it—that never, never, never could I let it go; only she thought it was the houses and the kitchen ranges and the linen and china, when it was really all the human souls to be saved" (p. 444).

Though Barbara has not the innocent sanctity of the conventional melodramatic heroine, she is intended as Shaw's equivalent in the line. He wrote to Eleanor Robson, "You see, the priest Keegan in John Bull was an immense success (I mean inside myself, though he did very well on the stage); and now I want to see whether I can make a woman a saint too."[7] But Barbara's sanctity is no more con-

---

[6] Of course Undershaft lusts for Barbara's soul ("I shall hand on my torch to my daughter. She shall make my converts and preach my gospel—" p. 287); but Shaw uses Cusins, who thinks in terms of Greek tragedy, to reconcile Undershaft the father with Undershaft the seducer:

CUSINS. Have you, too, fallen in love with Barbara?
UNDERSHAFT. Yes, with a father's love.
CUSINS. A father's love for a grown-up daughter is the most dangerous of all infatuations. I apologize for mentioning my own pale, coy, mistrustful fancy in the same breath with it (p. 286).

[7] *The Fabric of Memory,* p. 39.

ventionally passionless than it is conventionally innocent. It is not
the divinity hedging the usual pure-minded heroine of Melodrama
which enables Barbara to subdue the brutality and violence of
Bill Walker. Rather it is force of will and confidence in oneself
and one's mission. Barbara's foil, the more conventionally virginal
Jenny Hill, has no such protection when Bill Walker behaves in
the style of Bill Sikes . . . or Danny Mann drowning Eily O'Connor
in *The Colleen Bawn*. Bill strikes down old Rummy Mitchens and
seizes Jenny Hill by the hair *"so violently that she also screams."*
He holds Jenny *"writhing in his grasp . . . she screams again as
he wrenches her head down"*; she asks God for strength, Bill meanwhile *"striking her with his fist in the face."* No providential retribution like that which overtook Sikes or Danny Mann saves Jenny
Hill, though the subject of retribution is not ignored and the melo-
dramatics of the scene create an appropriate background for a con-
sideration of the ethics and efficacy of vengeance. Barbara's handling
of Bill gains much from the contrast with his treatment of Jenny;
and the difference between her sanctity and that of the conventional
innocent heroine is rendered unmistakable.

Undershaft has other associations with the villainous heavies of
Melodrama besides those related to his designs on Barbara. He is
given the manner and force of the conventional heavy (see Shaw's in-
structions to the actor, pp. 32–33 above); he has the mesmeric power
of the type, and when *"He suddenly reaches up and takes Barbara's
hands, looking powerfully into her eyes,"* she answers *"hypnotized"*
(p. 482). He also recalls the merciless bankers and ruthless financiers
most notably represented by Gideon Bloodgood in Boucicault's *Streets
of London* (*Poor of New York*, N.Y., 1857), who ruins others in the
first act, "The Panic of 1837," and profits malevolently in the second,
"The Panic of 1857." Like Undershaft, Bloodgood will cheat, steal,
and attempt to kill rather than be poor, and he does all these things
successively. Bloodgood, however, is a villain because he is a villain,
whereas Undershaft deliberately adopts the style. Undershaft one day
decided "that nothing should stop me except a bullet, neither reason
nor morals nor the lives of other men. I said 'Thou shalt starve ere
I starve'; and with that word I became free and great. I was a dangerous man until I had my will: now I am a useful, beneficent, kindly
person. That is the history of most self-made millionaires, I fancy.
When it is the history of every Englishman we shall have an England
worth living in" (*Barbara*, p. 435). Undershaft makes a principle of
Bloodgood's lack of principle.

The conventional stage villain, however, was not content merely
to act villainously; he also professed villainy, as a code. He was not,
like Sartorius in *Widowers' Houses*, a man convinced that his actions

were reasonable, decent, and inevitable in the light of circumstances; he was consciously wicked and malevolent, hardening himself against the conscience which still caused him to start and shake, and occasionally uttering the devilish sentiments which were to call down upon him the wrath of heaven. Undershaft, preaching the devil's gospel of money and gunpowder, plays upon this convention for all it is worth, to the great scandal of Lady Britomart. In a "drama of unsettled ideals," Lady Britomart's conventional morality is given no initial advantage over Undershaft's heterodox morality; but to absolutists like Stephen, who believe that "Right is right; and wrong is wrong; and if a man cannot distinguish them properly, he is either a fool or a rascal" (p. 349), Undershaft's self-conscious turpitude is that of Richard Crookback, Macaire, and Spider Skinner, the gentlemanly scoundrel and master criminal in Jones and Herman's *Silver King*.

The *Silver King* (1882) was an expert Melodrama presenting an ideal division of the elements which are concentrated in the figure of Andrew Undershaft. It is a story of traduced and vindicated innocence, in which Wilfred Denver, who flees from a crime he mistakenly thinks his own, goes to Nevada and becomes the "Silver King." Meanwhile the true villain, Spider Skinner, has also been prospering, without qualm or conscience. He is impervious to the pleas of his own wife when he decides to evict Denver's temporarily destitute "widow" and "orphans" from their miserable cottage:

> *Olive.* But it isn't her fault she is poor.
> *Skinner.* Fault! It's no fault in England to be poor. It's a crime. That's the reason I'm rich.[8]

Undershaft uses the very language of Spider Skinner; and if Skinner is a master-thief and a murderer, Undershaft is a capitalist and a maker of aerial battleships, which to Shaw was the social equivalent. But Undershaft leaves no room for Olive's retort ("Rich? When I think how our money is got, I grudge the poorest labourer's wife her crust of bread and drink of water"):

> *Cusins.* Do you call poverty a crime?
> *Undershaft.* The worst of crimes. All the other crimes are virtues beside it: all the other dishonors are chivalry itself by comparison. Poverty blights whole cities; spreads horrible pestilences; strikes dead the very souls of all who come within sight, sound, or smell of it. What you call crime is nothing: a murder here and a theft there, a blow now and a

[8] H. A. Jones and Henry Herman, *The Silver King*, in *Representative Plays by Henry Arthur Jones* (Boston, 1925), I, p. 45.

curse then: what do they matter? they are only the accidents and illnesses of life. . . . (p. 434)

The paradoxical inversion of crime and disease, crime and misfortune, is originally Erewhonian. But to propound it as a gospel in a play, Shaw creates Undershaft in the image, not of Butler's conscientious traveller, but of the Prince of Darkness and his melodramatic counterparts.

Skinner's principles, or rather, his articulate lack of principle, do not spare him from working hard at his "profession" for his money. He is rich, but not so rich as Undershaft, who can afford to relax into the role of the beneficent, kindly millionaire, who creates a heavenly city for his workmen in England's green and pleasant land, resulting incidentally in "a colossal profit, which comes to me." The benevolent millionnaire in *The Silver King* is Wilfred Denver, whose money came to him without effort and without stain; who

> . . . went to bed one night a common miner, and the next a millionaire.
> *Selwyn.* I've heard so. They call him the Silver King.
> *Baxter.* Gives a lot of money away, doesn't he?
> *Selwyn.* His whole life is spent in doing good. He's as noble and generous as he is rich. (p. 69)

Denver even speaks of the city in Nevada that he, like Undershaft, has built, "where every man would shed his blood for me, and every child is taught to reverence the name of John Franklin [Denver's pseudonym]."

The diabolism of Skinner, the anti-social villain, and the humanitarian paternalism of Denver, the benevolent millionaire, are the nicely distinguished melodramatic references for Andrew Undershaft, humanitarian diabolist and self-declared mystic bent on making power for the world, who would have every man do as he had done and become dangerous, and whose vocation in the end is the same as Barbara's: the saving of souls.[9]

The difference between the use of Melodrama in *The Devil's Disciple* and in *Major Barbara* is in the integrity of the stage world

[9] Shaw looked upon Blake as the great visionary poet-prophet of moral and social revolution and of creative evolution, and in these respects, his own direct ancestor. Undershaft's diabolism is Blake's diabolism, as Shaw understood it: the form taken by Blake's rejection of encrusted and perverted idealities. Dick Dudgeon in *The Devil's Disciple* similarly dramatized the rejection of his mother's puritanism with a dash of brimstone; but the melodramatic course of events reveals to him that his seeming irreligion is a higher religion. Undershaft is of course aware of the two sides of his gospel, the destructive and the visionary. It is up to Barbara and the others to discover the visionary, creative side if they can.

that the genre conventions create. In *The Devil's Disciple,* Melodrama provided a form and a method, and the play is a demonstration of what can be done within the genre. In *Major Barbara,* Melodrama provides a center of suggestive associations, and the form and method of the play belong outside the genre. The conventions of Melodrama are used casually, impressionistically. In the long run, however, Melodrama with its broad effects, strong narrative interests, and ideal types, though easily harnessed to project its own form of the Drama of Ideas, was scarcely compatible with the subtly analytical and discursive techniques of the Discussion Play. That *Major Barbara* falls into two distinct halves, two distinct keys, suggests that it should be regarded (presumably without disparagement) as "experimental" or as "transitional" between two mature modes, between *The Devil's Disciple, Captain Brassbound,* and the Melodrama of Ideas, and *Getting Married, Misalliance,* and the Discussion.

Major Barbara: Shaw's "Divine Comedy"

by Joseph Frank

Major Barbara can be considered the epitome of Shaw's total dramatic output. It embodies most of the social ideas and stage techniques of his earlier plays, and it distinctly foreshadows the ideology of the remaining four decades of his literary life. Moreover, *Major Barbara* is probably Shaw's most religious work; certainly it is the play of his which deals most explicitly with the threefold theme of sin, repentance, and salvation. (*Back to Methuselah* is less explicit, more diluted, as a play about religion.) Hence to label *Major Barbara* as Shaw's "Divine Comedy" is meant to be neither facetious nor hyperbolic, but to indicate a new point of departure from which to view the play. At the same time, to use the lens of the *Divine Comedy* to re-examine *Major Barbara* is not to imply that the two works are necessarily equal in artistic merit or that they are even fully comparable. Yet the Dantean perspective can, I think, help us to see Shaw's play in a new and brighter light, and by so doing clarify its central position in the Shavian canon as well as its possible stature as one of the great works of the twentieth century.

The most obvious objection to this method is the wide disparity between the *Divine Comedy* and *Major Barbara* as comedies. It is true that, in Dantean terms, each work is written in the vernacular, each has a happy ending. But here, insofar as the "comedy" is concerned, the resemblance ceases; and even here it is, at best, superficial. In Shaw's hands the vernacular, instead of becoming a matrix for lofty language, is utilized partly as an easy joke—witness Bill Walker's orthographic gymnastics—and partly as a trenchant instrument for probing the evils of democratic capitalism. In addition, the happy ending of Shaw's play is, in its implications, far more ambiguous, far less triumphant, than Dante's finale.

The comedic differences between the two works extend much further. Shaw, as always in his plays, is sufficiently skilled and shrewd to

"Major Barbara: *Shaw's 'Divine Comedy'*" *by Joseph Frank. Reprinted by permission of the Modern Language Association of America from* Publications of the Modern Language Association, *LXXI (March, 1956), 61–74.*

incorporate many stage situations which are deliberately intended to evoke laughter—either a Hollywood guffaw or a West End titter. Dante's comic touches, on the other hand, represent only a relative relaxation of the serious, usually by intensifying the grotesque to the point where the laughter momentarily outweighs the horror, or by inserting brief humanizing interludes. Thus where Dante's occasional comic mask tends to be that of the grinning gargoyle or the compassionate saint, Shaw's more regular expression is that of the clown or the sophisticate; and thus the risible comedy in *Major Barbara,* though a part of the play's message, is somewhat less serious and less in harmony with its context than that of the *Divine Comedy.*

The relatively broad humor in the eighth circle of the Inferno, where barrators and demons gruesomely frolic in and around the boiling pitch, is fittingly macabre and sardonic. The equivalent, if less organic, humor in *Major Barbara*—that which is meant to evoke the guffaw—is based not on the grotesque but on the ridiculous, not on the intensification of partial horror but on the exaggeration of complete ineptitude. When Stephen "advises" his mother in the first act or when Lomax "explains" about high explosives in the last act, we laugh at the foolishness of two presumptuous males, not at the hint of a strangling silver cord or a dismembered Cholly. In such comparatively extraneous moments, Shaw, by means of obvious caricature, is trying to produce a response not unlike that intended by the Hollywood gag-writer—and often for the same box-office reasons.

The intellectual, or West End, jokes scattered throughout *Major Barbara*—those, that is, which are not part and parcel of the play's central theme—serve a relaxing function parallel to the humanizing touches in Dante. In the play, however, these "extra" laughs have essentially one form and one motif: the sophisticated parody of the well-made, idea-less drawing room comedy. Thus the superficial plot structure of *Major Barbara*, with its contrived, almost distorted, happy ending, pokes fun at a chronic stage tradition. Then, too, the fact that the inheritor of Undershaft's business and the husband of his daughter must be a foundling—literally, a bastard—enables Shaw subtly to mock many of the conventions of standard upper-bracket comedy. On a deeper level, only when Cusins becomes a self-avowed bastard can he become a worthy successor to Undershaft and a worthy mate for Barbara; but Cusins' lesser role—as the foundling hero in the "happy" plot—is an evident parody of the heroes of Scribe and of Scribe's many descendants.

These ingredients of the guffaw and the titter are, however, the trappings of Shaw's play, the well-learned tricks of his trade—just as, for instance, the travelogue and dream features are the somewhat extraneous appurtenances of Dante's poem. In no sense, then, can Shaw's surface comedy elicit the adjective "divine." What divinity *Major Barbara* does have lies instead in its dominant religiousness and, through this, in its marked structural similarities to Dante's epic. Each work moves from sin to repentance to salvation, from the pit of hell to the vision of heaven. Each work has a cosmic theme and an inexorable internal logic. Despite the customary picture of Shaw as buffoon and agnostic, each work is a devoutly serious parable of the human predicament.

Even so, no real parallelism between the two works can be observed until the second act of *Major Barbara*—provided that we, like the play's original audience, ignore the rather redundant and patronizing preface. But where Dante takes only a single canto to get launched on his ascent of the mountain of medieval theology, Shaw requires almost an entire act to prepare for his descent into the valley of modern society. Hence the first act of *Major Barbara* serves mainly to introduce the characters; only indirectly does it deal with the themes of sin and repentance which dominate Act ii, and with the vision of salvation which is the moral of Act iii. None the less, after Lady Brit has given her son Stephen a functional exposition of the family problems and thereby prepared us to meet the rest of the household, and after Undershaft has been literally introduced to his own children, Shaw, shortly before the end of the first act, lets his audience know that the comedy they are seeing is also to be a religious allegory.

Almost from their first appearance the two leading characters are obviously concerned with religion: it is their vocation, and the terminology of that vocation gives their speeches an increasingly theological, if often paradoxical, flavor. Barbara is a faithful servant of the Salvation Army. Undershaft is a merchant of blood and fire—but the blood more and more suggests some kind of sacrament, and the fire the cleansing cauldron of a Shavian purgatory. Since both daughter and father are self-assured, articulate, and enthusiastically evangelical, it is inevitable that they challenge each other to a proselytizing contest: the Salvation shelter versus the cannon foundry. Each confidently accepts the match, and the curtain falls on Act i to the off-stage accompaniment of "Onward, Christian Soldiers."

The remaining two acts of *Major Barbara* go on to exhibit an ideological structure which, though almost antipodal in content to that of the *Divine Comedy,* is ironically very like Dante's in its underlying form. In both cases this underlying form is rigidly logical: if one accepts the authors' first premises, the intellectual edifices which they erect appear to be airtight and imposing. But where Dante had as his teachers Aquinas and the Universal Church, Shaw had Marx and the Fabian Society. Dante's first premise is, therefore, the absolute justice of an omnipotent God; Shaw's, the sinfulness of poverty. If either of these two premises is granted, the work constructed upon it has all the strength inherent in a valid syllogism. Since, however, Shaw's opening act is largely introductory, Act II of *Major Barbara* has to serve a multiple function: it clearly states the author's basic premise, and it proceeds to illustrate the horrors of Shavian sin and to indicate the proper road to Shavian salvation—and thus it includes much of the equivalent material found in the Inferno and Purgatorio.

Yet the setting of Shaw's second act is not the nine circles of the Inferno, but the square yard of a West Ham Salvation Army shelter; not a scene of intemperance, violence, and fraud, but the wretched, sin-breeding limbo of poverty. Nor are the denizens of this ostensibly merciful hell the unrepentant victims of human pride: Snobby Price and Rummy Mitchens, not Boniface and Ulysses, are here confined— the abject products of human humility, guilty of the sin of being poor. Until Undershaft arrives on the scene, Shaw is without a Virgil; therefore the servility and degradation and hypocrisy of poverty are at first allowed to speak for themselves, without comment, without interpretation. When the deserving unemployed painter, Peter Shirley, comes into the shelter, he, like the unbaptized infant souls at the outer rim of Dante's Inferno, merely italicizes the rigidity of a system wherein the action of crime—here, poverty—calls forth the equal reaction of punishment—here, the debilitating charity of the Salvation Army.

But, as both Dante and Shaw are at pains to point out, proper repentance can mitigate sin. Thus early in the second act Shaw's cockney Cato, Bill Walker, enters the scene and promptly strikes Jenny Hill, a young and innocent Salvation Army lass. Thereafter, Act II involves two simultaneous actions: that taking place within the microcosmic hell of the shelter itself, and the purgatorial struggle within the conscience of Bill Walker. The fact that Bill seems to rise as Barbara seems to fall not only gives this act a tight chiasmic structure, but dramatically reveals the interrelation of its two major motifs, sin and repentance—for Jenny's smashed face is Shaw's first step in leading his cast, and his audience, along the path to salvation.

Sin is the first of these motifs to be fully displayed. Undershaft, almost immediately upon coming onstage, announces that he is a "confirmed mystic" whose religion consists of being a millionaire. Within the play Undershaft is both Shaw's Virgilian spokesman and the Christ and Paul of this Shavian religion. As such, he is articulately proud of his million-fold removal from sin and his state of earnest self-salvation rather than lazy infamy. When Shirley remonstrates that he wouldn't have Undershaft's conscience for all his income, Undershaft replies, "I wouldn't have your income, not for all your conscience." The ethical battle, in which both Barbara and Cusins temporarily join ranks with Shirley, has thus begun: the proselytizing contest is under way.

Cusins is Undershaft's first major antagonist. But since, at this point in the play, Cusins has all the diffidence of the "collector of religions," he does not put up much resistance. To his question, "Is there any place in your religion for honor, justice, truth, love, mercy and so forth?" Undershaft replies with a qualified Yes: these qualities "are the graces and luxuries of a rich, strong, and safe life," but without money and gunpowder they are merely unattainable graces and luxuries.

Despite Cusins' apparent lack of aggressiveness in this ethical battle, Shaw seems to have loaded the dice in his favor and against his own spokesman. Undershaft is no prince of peace, no ascetic socialist, not even a faithful Fabian, but an unscrupulous capitalist who thrives on war, a literal merchant of death. For a moment it looks as if the argument will end in a rout, as if Shaw, the purported exhibitionistic jester always willing to sacrifice logic and consistency for the sake of a funny paradox, has here put himself in the dilemma of supporting either self-evident social evil or the most blatant form of capitalism. But Undershaft is not only a confirmed mystic and millionaire; like all the founders of the world's religions he has also led an appropriately holy life. Hence, as he proceeds to make clear, money and gunpowder symbolize freedom and power as well as the fitting crown to his own earthly endeavors. Money and gunpowder, because he now controls both in abundance, have made him a free and powerful man, for they have enabled him to rise above servitude and weakness, above poverty. The ruthlessness of his scramble to get above the common level is thus an indication of the fervor of his religious motivation.

Can we say, then, that Undershaftianity is the code of the Robber Barons—a scheme of capitalist apologetics? This is the core of Barbara's argument when she, replacing Cusins, insists that her father, with all his money, cannot buy the Salvation Army—a true religion because its "blood" is the militant blood of Christ and its "fire" the joyous zeal of doing God's work among the cold and dispossessed. But Bodger the distiller and Undershaft the warmonger do succeed in buying the Salvation Army—using, incidentally, the same "tainted" money which Shaw analyzed in his first play, *Widowers' Houses,* and which, forty years later, he reconsidered in his *Too True to Be Good.* Moreover, not only are Bodger and Undershaft successful in purchasing Barbara's church, but presumably they will go on using it as an effective weapon to subvert any resistance to their form of capitalism. Thus at first glance Shaw seems to be saying that Undershaftianity is only the richer and shrewder of two equally false religions. The fact that Act II ends with Barbara on the verge of tears implies that, while she has been defeated, her father has not triumphed.

Yet Shaw, through Undershaft, has anticipated Barbara's only partial capitulation, for it is her soul—like that of Everyman or of Dante himself—over which the forces of good and evil are to engage in ultimate conflict. Hence, in the middle of the second act, Undershaft, just before he tells Cusins that he is able to buy the Salvation Army, announces that the three of them—Barbara, Cusins, and himself—"must stand together above the common people: how else can we help their children to climb up beside us?" The Shaw who was later to flirt with Mussolini and Stalin, who was to become increasingly bitter in his attacks on democracy, was thereby declaring both a dramatic and a political or theological principle: dramatic in that Barbara's conversion, in the context of the play's broad allegory, will represent the conversion of all enlightened people; and political or theological in that Shaw's brave new world, the Undershaftian city of God, can be achieved only by a revolution led by the elite. In this way Undershaft's metaphysic, which is clarified in the third act, is at least projected in the second act—by both the characterization and the utterances of its founder and chief prophet. Even so, at this point in the play the Undershaftian gospel is still largely negative and indirect, destructive and amorphous—still, potentially, the self-justifying code of the successful Robber Baron.

Repentance, however, is the other dominant motif of Act II; and Bill Walker's remorse, despite its gutter dialect, is as important to the drama as Undershaft's preliminary dialectics. The latter's success in purchasing the Salvation Army makes it seem, as the curtain descends, as though Barbara's soul has been plunged into purgatory, Bill's released. But her purgatory is to be relatively private and temporary— her interlude of loneliness and indecision before final conversion; while his purgatory, despite his ostensibly jaunty exit, is to be relatively public and enduring—his apparent acceptance of a religious and social system in which expiation, because it is either superficial or vindictive, does not promote Shavian salvation.

Specifically, Walker's problem is this—and Shaw dramatizes it with exuberant if disciplined gusto. Bill has struck an innocent girl across the face. Under sufficient prodding from Barbara he begins to feel remorse. This is an uncomfortable feeling, one he would like to be rid of. In two ways, therefore, he tries to get rid of it: by buying forgiveness through giving money to the church, and by compensating for his crime through getting himself struck across the face. But the Salvation Army will not take his money, and Todger Fairmile uses him for a prayer mat rather than a punching bag. Hence his remorse persists. Presumably, had the church accepted his pound or had Todger Fairmile hit him harder than he hit Jenny, then Bill would have been cleared: he could again strike Jenny, offer his pound or his jaw to pay for the blow, and thus, with a clear conscience, repeat the cycle. But since he is unable to atone for the obvious crime of beating up a young and innocent girl, he must go on feeling miserable; and because such a feeling is uncomfortable he will be unlikely to commit a similar crime. Still, Walker is more than willing to "get" Rummy Mitchens, for she, by threatening to "av the lor [law] of him," has allowed him to feel that, so far as she is concerned, he is competing fairly in society's vicious and retaliatory game of external punishment.

When, at the end of Act II, Cusins ironically announces that "the millennium will be inaugurated by the unselfishness of Undershaft and Bodger," and when Barbara has seen murder and drunkenness seemingly replace her God, Bill can ask cynically, "Wot prawce selvytion nah?" Yet, despite his cynicism, he has not been able to escape from his own feeling of remorse; he has only seen that the church and its missionaries are, essentially, no more moral than himself. In the double sense that he has not fully atoned for his crime and that he still accepts the archaic code of an eye for an eye, he is in Shaw's purgatory; but in the double sense that he is less likely to commit a similar crime and that he has begun to question society's method of imposing justice, he is on the road to salvation.

Does not much of Bill Walker's role, however, seem to contradict the rest of the play's ideology? If poverty is the worst of sins, and if the gospel of St. Andrew Undershaft is the road to heaven, how does Walker's problem of personal expiation fit in? Shaw's answer, provided largely in the play's final act, indicates the tightness of *Major Barbara*'s logic. The Salvation Army, as we see it in Act II, is both morally and theologically the noblest extant example of Christianity because it is the most joyous, energetic, and broadly evangelical of the Christian churches. But because, according to Shaw, it shows its religious lineage and present social context by preaching the acceptance of the earthly status quo, it fosters the prime sin of poverty, as well as the closely related sins of humility and submission. Through both its doctrine of vicarious atonement and its reactionary function in modern society it substitutes the collection plate and the policeman's club for genuine and productive remorse. In order for humanity to create a city of God devoid of the sin of poverty, man must slough off his humility and submission, must cultivate the virtues of pride and rebellion. This he cannot do if he accepts the "mercanto-Christian morality" wherein either Christ atones for our sins or society balances our crimes with external punishments. Bill Walker's remorse is thus the first step in his becoming a social revolutionist. Though he does not appear in Act III, the play's final scene reveals what he has to gain by substituting Undershaftianity for what Shaw calls Crosstianity—while *Heartbreak House* shows what Bill has to lose if he persists in his cynicism.

This final scene—after Stephen in the first scene of Act III has underlined the smugness, decadence, and feebleness of British democratic capitalism—presents the Shavian city of God. Says Cusins, as the scene opens, "It needs only a cathedral to be a heavenly city instead of a hellish one." Perivale St. Andrews does, in fact, contain several churches. Consequently, the paradox—what Barbara had earlier referred to as the "frightful irony" of her father's factory of death—is at once geometric and monumental: the allegedly heavenly city is the source of death and destruction. Nor does its Machiavellian owner care who wins in the wars from which he now profits. The Undershaft enterprise is, in short, the embodiment of war, imperialism, and ruthless capitalism. Yet the houses of this factory town are clean and comfortable, the workers happy and well-fed. Here is no sign of poverty. Hence, if nothing else, the factory of death is also a materialistic Utopia. Undershaft, its manager, its administrative god, begins to resolve this paradox when he first describes the community in terms of organized efficiency: as the attempt, on a small scale, to reorganize human life so that it contains a minimum of trouble and anxiety, and, as a result, so that it produces a maximum of the world's material goods.

But the paradox appears to be intensified, not resolved, if these material "goods" are such obvious evils as aerial battleships and ingenious high explosives. Undershaftianity, for all its gloss, seems for the moment the code of an international bandit that would make the depredations of the Robber Barons look like the felonies of a pickpocket. It is at this point, with Undershaft on one side and Barbara and Cusins on the other, that the final battle for the heroine's soul commences. This battle is divided into two parts: first, will Undershaft be able to bridge what Cusins calls "the abyss of moral horror" between aerial battleships and the traditions of Western culture? second, if so, will Cusins and Barbara be able to cross that bridge? The abyss is wide, for Cusins, as a teacher of Greek, represents the best in Epicureanism, Barbara the best in Christian altruism; and the distance between Matthew Arnold, for instance, and Andrew Undershaft seems almost infinite.

Shaw does not brood long on this vast abyss, but having already made it pregnant in Act II, he now, through Undershaft, quickly but logically begins to build the sections of his bridge. The first of these is the postulate that the weapons of power are themselves amoral—hence the armorer's motto, "Unashamed," and hence the armorer's policy of giving arms to "all men who offer an honest price for them, without respect of persons or principles." On the basis of this creed, then, the weapons of destruction are available to the good as well as to the evil man.

The second section of the Shavian bridge starts to define the "good" man, though it does so in negative terms. He is not the exponent of the Salvation Army nor the inhabitant of Dante's Paradise: such a person is the product of an obsolete morality and an obsolete religion. In contrast, the "good" man is he who is willing to "scrap [the world's] . . . old prejudices and its old moralities and its old religions and its old political constitutions." To get part way across the bridge, therefore, the disciple of Undershaftianity must be willing to use violence, and to use it as the hammer of the iconoclast.

Shaw's third section crosses the middle of the abyss and, perhaps, marks an ascent. He who follows in the steps of a master must accept certain key teachings of that master. Undershaft's own life story— which is now employed as a parable within a parable—illustrates some of these teachings. His disciple must view poverty as the worst of sins, and he must hold this view so strongly that he is willing to destroy and kill in order to eradicate it. The ruthlessness of Undershaft's rise above poverty here points up Shaw's conviction that, in the area of basic morality, the end does justify the means—as in Dante the means, the death of hope in the Inferno, is justified by the end, the exaltation of the Paradiso. But Undershaft's materialistic success in life is not intended to convey only a negative creed; for Shaw's "good" man who is willing to use violence to break down outmoded beliefs and institutions must also desire to replace them with at least "the cleanliness and respectability" of Perivale St. Andrews: to replace the seven deadly sins of lack of money with the seven cardinal virtues of sufficient money for food, clothing, heat, rent, taxes, decency, and children, and to replace the charity of the Salvation Army with the security of economic equality.

Having taken Cusins and Barbara this far, Undershaft leaves the stage while they take the fourth and final step. He has shown them the means and some of the reasons for reorganizing modern society; it is now up to them either to supply positive and spiritual reasons for such a revolution or to renounce Undershaft's philosophy as brutal materialism. But the mephistophelian Undershaft, having seen Barbara nibble at the bait, goes into his office confident that his daughter and her prospective mate now know both good and evil, confident that they will be able to cross the bridge that stretches from the

Acropolis and Golgotha to the socialist world of tomorrow, and confident that they will become worthy instruments of that Life Force of which he feels himself a part.

In swallowing Undershaft's bait Barbara and Cusins in a very real sense move from an earthly paradise to a Shavian vision of heaven. If Perivale St. Andrews suggests Shaw's Garden of Eden, his threshold to heaven, then the final interlude of serious dialogue in the play, both in its content and in its attempt to heighten whatever lyricism has gone before, can be said to parallel, not parody, Dante's multifoliate rose. Yet this scene-within-a-scene begins in a matter-of-fact fashion with Cusins' announcement that he is going to accept Undershaft's offer to become his eventual successor, and Barbara's flat "I thought you would." Still matter-of-fact is the question which Cusins then immediately asks himself: has he merely sold his soul to get money and, possibly, Barbara? And still matter-of-fact are their answers: Cusins' that he has sold it for power—"to make power for the world," and Barbara's "I want to make power for the world too, but it must be spiritual power."

It is at this point that the tone of the play briefly changes. No longer the muted and ambiguous "Onward, Christian Soldiers" of the end of Act I, nor the sardonic "Olympian diapason" with which Cusins celebrates the descent of Dionysos Undershaft just before the end of Act II. The tone now becomes religious and soaring. At first the dialogue is contrapuntal, then it rises to a single melody. The counterpoint gathers momentum when Cusins asserts that all power is potentially spiritual and potentially available to all men. Then Barbara replies that such power as they see around them—"Power to burn down women's houses and kill their sons and tear their husbands to pieces" —is evil. To which Cusins answers: "You cannot have power for good without having power for evil," and the power manufactured at Perivale St. Andrews is potentially good—"simple enough for common men to use, yet strong enough to force the intellectual oligarchy to use its genius for the general good." And so, as Barbara accepts Cusins' decision to don the Undershaft mantle, the counterpoint comes to an end.

It is she who then carries the burden of the melody. Starting in a minor key she first laments that there is no alternative—turning one's back on Bodger and Undershaft is turning one's back on life. Barbara, the granddaughter of a peer, the daughter of a foundling, belongs to all classes and to no class; and she who had immersed herself in "life" in the Salvation Army cannot now shirk her duty. Her own soul, having labored in hell, having gone through purgatory, now sees its own mission clarified and extended, now, at last, sees Shaw's vision of God

—a vision which, if not beyond the sun and the stars, is at least no longer earthbound. That duty, that vision, is the true saving of human souls:

> Not weak souls in starved bodies, sobbing with gratitude for a scrap of bread and treacle, but fullfed, quarrelsome, snobbish, uppish creatures, all standing on their little rights and dignities. . . . That is where salvation is really wanted. My father shall never throw it in my teeth again that my converts were bribed with bread. [She is transfigured.] I have got rid of the bribe of bread. I have got rid of the bribe of heaven. Let God's work be done for its own sake: the work he had to create us to do because it cannot be done except by living men and women. When I die, let him be in my debt, not I in his; and let me forgive him as becomes a woman of my rank.
>
> *Cusins.* Then the way of life lies through the factory of death?
> *Barbara.* Yes, through the raising of hell to heaven and of man to God, through the unveiling of an eternal light in the Valley of The Shadow.

Like Dante's pilgrim, Shaw's Barbara has momentarily become one with that cosmic Will which, through its human agents, can transform the factory of death into the city of life. The play is over; and so, after a few lines of down-to-earth horseplay, the curtain falls.

But has it fallen on a Divine Comedy or on a fuzzy mixture of farce and Fascism? On the former, I think, for *Major Barbara* has much more in common with Dante than with Van Druten or d'Annunzio. The play's basic seriousness is indicated, if not proved, by its centrality to Shaw's prolific dramatic output. In the simplest terms, *Major Barbara* incorporates the socialistic message of many of Shaw's earlier comedies and the disillusion with democracy of his later plays. It pays brief homage to the Life Force mystique which was to dominate his plays for the next twenty years, but in giving this Force a definitely subsidiary role Shaw also foreshadows his own partial shedding of this belief in his final productions. On the more technical level, his treatment of Undershaft utilizes the same attitude of light mockery and deep reverence which marks Shaw's portrayal of the hero—from Mrs. Warren and Dick Dudgeon, through Caesar and St. Joan, to the kings of *The Apple Cart* and *In Good King Charles's Golden Days*. At the same time, his parody of existing stage practices in *Major Barbara* is not unlike that in, for instance, *Arms and the Man* or *The Millionairess*. In short, both the play's message and its method represent an epitome of Shaw's career as a playwright. Only by viewing that whole career as trivial can *Major Barbara* be dismissed as unworthy of serious attention. Nor does the play's specific meaning—regardless of how offensive we may find its call to revolution, its economic radicalism, its undemocratic faith in an elite, and its scorn of traditional religions and institutions—suggest that it is either fuzzy or tongue-in-cheek. For *Major Barbara* is almost certainly the work of a serious artist at the height of his powers, an artist who is trying by every means at his command to deliver a meaningful and convincing message.

Dante's message, however, has long provided a penetrating and artistic insight into the medieval period. Can Shaw's play make any such claims for the twentieth century? Here any similarity between Dante and Shaw is, at best, a matter of conjecture; yet to claim that a parallel exists is, I think, by no means absurd. Dante's inclusive theology not only ranged the cosmos, but it comprehended the politics and economics, as well as the psychology and ethics, of his own era. Moreover, Dante's philosophy, whether dated or divine, is still provocative in its message and convincing in its artistry. In terms of intent, *Major Barbara* is equally inclusive: its subject matter extends to the same fields, its time span is both the present and the future, and its dramatis personae, like that of the *Divine Comedy,* is meant to include all men. Thus Shaw's attempt at Dantean scope can, it seems to me, be granted.

Yet breadth without depth is pretentiousness. Does *Major Barbara,* then, dissect as well as display the problems of our own century? To try to answer this question fully involves bringing in matters which lie outside this discussion, but it is perhaps relevant to point out that since 1905, the year in which the play was written, England has experienced a general strike and a major depression, not to mention two socialistic prime ministers. Since then, too, as it is almost unnecessary to remind ourselves, the Victorian promise has been shaken if not shattered by two world wars, by the rise of Fascism and Communism, and by the possibility of the imminent suicide of the human race. These events, both major and minor, at least indicate that, in Undershaft's words, we are still faced with the problem of "organizing civilization." In any such organization the constituent problems of the role of capitalism, the function of the so-called strong man, the readiness of humanity for democracy, and the nature of a "modern" religion must all be considered. In the half-century since *Major Barbara* was first produced these specific problems have become more, not less, demanding; and hence, in terms of the questions it examines, Shaw's comedy cannot yet be called dated.

Even so, many sturdy works of didactic art have perished because their solutions to the problems which they raise have become morally or pragmatically irrelevant. This is particularly true of those works which take an extreme or doctrinaire stand—and Dante has probably survived in spite of some of his theological excesses. Shaw, in using Undershaft as his spokesman and in pitting the Salvation Army against a munitions factory, has obviously chosen not to follow an ideological via media. In fact, the play's iconoclasm and mysticism are, in combination, an almost sure prescription for excess. That *Major Barbara* takes a stand at once extreme and doctrinaire is therefore not surprising. But the question remains: is that stand still relevant and still worthy of attention?

Dante's era—like ours—was characterized by the overriding importance of its institutions. Yet where Dante, despite his historical context, emphasizes the primacy of individual salvation through personal righteousness, Shaw states that the reform of society's economic life must come first. In an age where the individual as an individual seems to be becoming increasingly powerless, it is highly probable that institutional reform should take precedence. This suggests, however, that human behavior is dependent on external circumstances—a belief which can all too easily lead to the dead-end of determinism (and to the neglect of art). Shaw is explicitly aware of this danger, and he takes considerable pains in *Major Barbara* to show how the individual is personally responsible for the reform of his institutions.

As he makes clear in Bill Walker's remorse and in Barbara's conversion, there is no readily bought forgiveness, nor is there any redemption from our sins by a Christ who died on the cross to atone for them or who promised to redeem our earthly misery in an eternal heaven; for we can only truly expiate our sins by ceasing to sin. In addition, there is no inexorable pattern of history which will guarantee the proper reorganization of civilization. Shaw scorns rather than loves the proletariat, and the play's three leading characters are pointedly classless. Nor are the capitalists themselves evil demons who will necessarily be crushed by the relentless forward march of the new society. In brief, Shaw, just as he shuns a reliance on the retaliatory justice of society or on the sweeping forgiveness of God, renounces any sort of faith in Marxian determinism. This is his negative way of insisting on individual responsibility.

He also insists on individual responsibility in a positive manner. Shaw's superman is the person who has a sharp and true view of reality—be that person devout saint, ruthless warmonger, pragmatic student of the classics, or enlightened theatregoer. When Undershaft converts Barbara and Cusins, he is, in Shaw's sense, converting them to realism. It is true that this form of realism is something only for the elite: because neither God nor history nor society itself will accomplish the organization of civilization, and because the masses are cowed and apathetic, the superman must take the lead in reforming society. He must first recognize and then abolish civilization's fundamental sin of poverty, and then he must give to civilization a vision of something beyond bread and treacle. This is Shavian realism. Therefore, despite the fact that Shaw's primary concern is with society and not with humanity, it is the elite who alone can assume the responsibility for making society humane and, eventually, godly. Only after civilization has been so organized, says Shaw, can the average individual become truly free and responsible.

But, fundamentally, the question of whether or not civilization follows Shaw's advice is irrelevant to the intrinsic worth of *Major Barbara*—and Dante has managed to survive in an essentially alien age. When Shaw, at the end of his preface to the play, expressed the hope that it was both true and inspired, he was probably just giving vent to the normal wish of most authors and all honest reformers. Even so, the truth and inspiration of *Major Barbara*, like the truth and inspiration of the *Divine Comedy*, almost certainly lie in the fact that the play is central to the message of an intensely serious and perceptive artist. Ultimately it is in this sense, and not in the way in which society accepts or rejects Shaw's diagnosis, that *Major Barbara* is likely long to remain relevant and worthy of deep attention.

Assault on Idealism: *Major Barbara*

by *Anthony S. Abbott*

> Well, you have made for yourself something that you call a
> morality or a religion or what not. It doesn't fit the facts. Well,
> scrap it. Scrap it and get one that does.
>
> Andrew Undershaft in *Major Barbara*

Despite the success of *The Devil's Disciple* in America, as late as
1903 Shaw was still having trouble getting his plays produced in
London. Three major plays, *Candida, Caesar and Cleopatra,* and the
newly completed *Man and Superman,* had yet to be publicly per-
formed. In 1904, however, an event occurred that was to completely
reverse the course of Shaw's fortunes. Harley Granville-Barker, in association with J. E. Vedrenne, became the manager of the Royal
Court Theatre. Barker, who knew and admired Shaw's work, accepted
the post at the Court only on the condition that he be allowed to
supplement the regular evening performances with a series of matinees
of Shaw's plays. As a result Shaw became "known" almost overnight.
During the four years of the Barker-Vedrenne management at the
Court eleven plays by Shaw received a total of 701 performances.[1]
"From that time," to quote Sir Lewis Casson, "Shaw was sure of his
market. He no longer had to try and make his plays saleable to the
normal commercial managements, but could write to please himself." [2]
The first play that Shaw wrote specifically for the Court Theatre
was *Major Barbara,* a work that only Granville-Barker would have
dared to produce or had the ability to direct. Frankly experimental
in form and daring in theme, *Major Barbara* is the first of Shaw's

---

"Assault on Idealism: Major Barbara*" by Anthony S. Abbott. From* Shaw and
Christianity *by Anthony S. Abbott (New York: The Seabury Press, 1965). Copyright © 1965 by The Seabury Press, Inc. Reprinted by permission of the publisher.*

[1] For further details see Raymond Mander and Joe Mitchenson, *Theatrical Companion to Shaw* (New York: Pitman, 1955), pp. 287–88.
[2] Sir Lewis Casson, "Granville-Barker, Shaw and the Court Theatre," *Theatrical
Companion,* p. 289.

dramas to illustrate his thesis that an effective play may be created purely from the clash of ideas. There are indications, particularly from Napoleon's long speech on the English in *The Man of Destiny* and from the detachable third acts of *Caesar and Cleopatra* and *Man and Superman,* that Shaw was anxious to break away from the confining techniques of the well-made play, but his primary technique during the '90's, as we have seen from *The Devil's Disciple,* was to give uncommon twists to conventional theatrical devices. Rebellion against convention is nonetheless preoccupation with it; parody and satire have their limitations as vehicles for philosophical thought, particularly when the playwright wishes to propound new ideas instead of ridiculing old ones. New thoughts, then, require new forms; and with the external obstacles to production at last removed, Shaw could now risk an experiment in that direction.*

Major Barbara is a discussion in three acts, each of which is almost a one-act play in itself. The first act is a drawing-room comedy in which the Philistine world of Wilton Crescent, represented by Lady Britomart, Stephen, Sarah, and Lomax, is exposed by the realist Undershaft and the two idealists, Barbara and Cusins. The second act is a presentation of several kinds of religious conflict in highly realistic, almost melodramatic, fashion. The near triumph of Barbara's Christian idealism over the stubborn Bill Walker and the eventual defeat of her faith by Undershaft's realistic worldliness form the emotional climax of the play. The focus of the third act, in contrast, is intellectual. The question of religious faith is debated in a symbolic world of futuristic mechanical conveniences, and atmospheric realism is totally abandoned for a series of symbols which illustrate Undershaft's philosophical position. The thin thread of plot which ties together the social satire of Act I, the religious melodrama of Act II, and the intellectual debate of Act III is the agreement between Barbara and her father that she will visit his munitions factory if he will visit her Salvation Army shelter.

More important than the plot as a motivating force for the action of the play is the clash of minds among the major characters. In *Major Barbara* Shaw is less interested in the response of characters to given situations than he is in the creation of conflicts between previously established ideological types. Conversion in *The Devil's Disciple* and *The Shewing-Up of Blanco Posnet* is only apparent, because

---

* Casson's reaction to Shaw's use of his new freedom is of interest. As a man of the theatre he decries Shaw's tendency, stemming from his success at the Court, "to over-emphasise the polemical in his plays at the expense of the character drawing and drama." (*Theatrical Companion,* p. 289.) He was also disturbed by Granville-Barker's decision to give up directing and play-writing for Shakespearean criticism.

Dick and Blanco merely respond to external circumstances by show-
ing their real natures. In *Major Barbara* conversion results from the
rational imposition of one ideology upon another. The abstract points
of view, particularly those of the three central figures, are actually
actors in the play in the sense that the mainspring of the play is the
clash of opinions rather than personalities.

The play opens in the citadel of fashionable London society, Wilton
Crescent. Shaw economically introduces his theme and takes care of
the necessary exposition by presenting Lady Britomart and her son
Stephen in an argument over the merits of the absent Andrew Undershaft. Lady Brit is quick to establish herself as a religious Philistine,
but unlike Mrs. Dudgeon, her counterpart in *The Devil's Disciple*,
she is no hypocrite. Intelligent, charming, and outspoken, she believes
in the values of her society and makes no pretense about it:

> I really cannot bear an immoral man. I am not a Pharisee, I hope; and
> I should not have minded his merely doing wrong things: we are none
> of us perfect. But your father didnt exactly do wrong things: he said
> them and thought them: that was what was so dreadful. He really had
> a sort of religion of wrongness. Just as one doesnt mind men practising
> immorality so long as they own that they are in the wrong by preaching
> morality; so I couldnt forgive Andrew for preaching immorality while
> he practised morality. You would all have grown up without principles,
> without any knowledge of right and wrong, if he had been in the house
> (pp. 348–49).

Though Lady Brit's distinction between morality and immorality is
based on her "conceiving the universe exactly as if it were a large
house in Wilton Crescent" (p. 341), the candor with which she admits
the limitations of the morality of her class makes her delightful, for
all her narrowness. She as much as admits that right and wrong mean
for her good taste and poor taste, and she consistently acts on this
assumption. When Undershaft and Barbara begin to discuss religion
toward the end of the act, she is shocked by their bad taste: "Really,
Barbara, you go on as if religion were a pleasant subject. Do have
some sense of propriety" (p. 362). Shaw does not treat Lady Brit's
form of irreligion too seriously, because she is quite harmless and can
be guaranteed to reduce all important matters to questions of taste.
For example, in the third act, when the long discussion about poverty,
morality, and munitions has deeply involved almost all the other
characters, she pays no attention whatever to the argument until her
sense of propriety forces her to speak: "Charles Lomax: you are a fool.
Adolphus Cusins: you are a Jesuit. Stephen: you are a prig. Barbara:
you are a lunatic. Andrew: you are a vulgar tradesman. Now you all
know my opinion; and my conscience is clear, at all events" (p. 439).
Stephen is a somewhat more dangerous type of religious Philistine

because, having neither the intelligence nor the wit of his mother, he takes himself very seriously. Having graduated from Harrow and Cambridge, he feels himself an expert on all moral questions and can say to his father with perfect philosophic gravity, "People may differ about matters of opinion or even about religion; but how can they differ about right and wrong? Right is right; and wrong is wrong: and if a man cannot distinguish them properly, he is either a fool or a rascal: that's all" (p. 349). The other two members of the Wilton Crescent set, Lomax and Sarah, are unimportant. Lomax is suspicious about the Salvation Army because it is not the Established Church, but he is too much of an idiot to articulate his ideas. Sarah appears to be purely decorative.

Shaw's method of criticizing this group is far more subtle than it had been in *The Devil's Disciple* or *The Shewing-Up of Blanco Posnet*. Dick Dudgeon directs a series of ironic thrusts at his mother and Blanco overwhelms his brother with abuse; but frontal attack is seldom employed in *Major Barbara*. Even when Undershaft berates Stephen or Lady Brit, he does so with the tone of an amused on-looker.* Lomax may rattle on senselessly about the virtues of the Church of England and Lady Brit may insist upon having her religion "in a proper and respectable way" without invoking blasts of criticism. Undershaft, Barbara, and Cusins simply ignore the others, for the most part, and leave them to condemn themselves by their own actions. Contrast, for example, the reading of the will in *The Devil's Disciple* with the following passage from the first act of the present play:

Lady Britomart. . . . Barbara is old enough to take her own way. She has no father to advise her.

Barbara. Oh yes she has. There are no orphans in the Salvation Army.

Undershaft. Your father there has a great many children and plenty of experience, eh?

Barbara (looking at him with quick interest and nodding). Just so. How did you come to understand that?

(Lomax is heard at the door trying the concertina.)

Lady Britomart. Come in, Charles. Play us something at once.

Lomax. Righto. *(He sits down in his former place and preludes.)*

Undershaft. One moment, Mr. Lomax. I am rather interested in the Salvation Army. Its motto might be my own: Blood and Fire (p. 359).

---

* Dick Dudgeon's first words to his mother upon entering the house are, "Well, mother: keeping up appearances as usual? thats right, thats right." *(Three Plays for Puritans,* p. 17.) Contrast this with Undershaft's almost shy, confused manner upon arriving at Lady Brit's.

With a single phrase, "One moment, Mr. Lomax," Undershaft quietly dispatches the Philistines, and the focus of the play has shifted. Undershaft, up to this point uneasy in the fashionable world of Wilton Crescent, quiet, almost conventional in manner, quickly comes to life. Barbara is surprised and fascinated by his reference to God, and he in turn is too interested in her work with the Salvation Army to endure Lomax any longer. The rest of the act is largely a discussion between Barbara and her father with periodic interruptions from the others. That the criticism of respectable religion is to be relegated to a subordinate position is soon clear. Barbara and Undershaft, ignoring the intrusions of the Philistines, quickly conclude their agreement, and the stage is set for the play's central theme, the clash between realism and idealism.

One of Shaw's favorite dramatic devices is the use of abrupt changes in tone like that between the first and second acts of *Major Barbara*. The figure of Stephen, stubbornly refusing to compromise his respectability, gives way to two figures having a meal in the yard outside the West Ham shelter of the Salvation Army. Through Bronterre O'Brien Price and Romola Mitchens, alias Snobby and Rummy, Shaw introduces the motif upon which variations will be played for the rest of the drama: the nature of salvation. As many as six different attitudes toward salvation are presented during the second act. There is the expiatory attitude of the Army upon which Snobby and Rummy play, the retaliatory ethic of Bill Walker, the pure Christian idealism of Barbara, the humility of Peter Shirley, the humanism of Cusins, and the realistic materialism of Undershaft.

It should be made clear at the outset that Shaw, in choosing the Salvation Army as the point around which to develop these variations, is not merely setting up a straw man which he will later demolish. During his cart-and-trumpet period [3] when he was making speeches for the Fabian Society in various parts of London, he became interested in the Army's work and its methods. Later on, as he told Archibald Henderson, when he was contemplating writing a play about the "conflict between the economic and religious views of life," [4] he turned to his knowledge of the Army as a source for his heroine's religious ideology. It is natural that Barbara, whose personality is dominated by a tremendous vitality, should choose as her spiritual outlet the Salvation Army with its motto of "Blood and Fire," and equally natural that Shaw, who so often criticized organized religion

[3] For further details on Shaw's knowledge of the Salvation Army during this period see Archibald Henderson, *George Bernard Shaw: Man of the Century* (New York: Appleton-Century-Crofts, 1956), p. 583 *n*.

[4] Archibald Henderson, *George Bernard Shaw: His Life and Works* (New York: Appleton, 1918), p. 381.

for its repressive qualities, should present the Army in a sympathetic light. Cusins, echoing Shaw's Preface, explains its merits to Undershaft:

> You do not understand the Salvation Army. It is the army of joy, of love, of courage: it has banished the fear and remorse and despair of the old hell-ridden evangelical sets: it marches to fight the devil with trumpet and drum, with music and dancing, with banner and palm, as becomes a sally from heaven by its happy garrison. It picks the waster out of the public house and makes a man of him: It finds a worm wriggling in a back kitchen, and lo! a woman! (p. 385).

Neither Barbara nor Cusins, however, is totally dedicated to the principles of the Army. Cusins has joined partly because he is Barbara's suitor and partly because, as a "collector of religions," he is excited by the Dionysiac element in the Army's approach to religion. With the actual work of conversion he seems to have no part. Barbara, though emotionally committed to the saving of souls, is in the words of Cusins "quite original in her religion" (p. 338). The difference between Barbara's Christianity and the Christianity of the Army is demonstrated by the contrast between her handling of Bill Walker and its treatment of Rummy Mitchens and Snobby Price.

The religious attitude of the Army is what Shaw terms "Salvationist" . . . and Rummy and Snobby are experts at the game of "Salvationism." The principle on which the Army works is simple: a man sins, he confesses his crimes and debaucheries at a public meeting, and having been purged of his guilt by his confession he is now "saved." The trouble with this system is that pretensions to contrition cannot be distinguished from sincere confessions. The Army, which must according to its principles accept a confession as genuine, is then at the mercy of the Rummy Mitchens and Snobby Prices of this world, who turn the ritual into a kind of confidence game:

> *Price.* Wot! Oh Rummy, Rummy! Respectable married woman, Rummy, gittin rescued by the Salvation Army by pretendin to be a bad un. Same old game!
> *Rummy.* What am I to do? I cant starve. Them Salvation lasses is dear good girls; but the better you are, the worse they likes to think you were before they rescued you. . . .
> *Rummy.* Who saved you, Mr. Price? Was it Major Barbara?
> *Price.* No: I come here on my own. I'm going to be Bronterre O'Brien Price, the converted painter. I know wot they like. I'll tell em how I blasphemed and gambled and wopped my poor old mother—(p. 368).

In the Hell Scene from *Man and Superman* Ana attempts much the same sort of thing. Surprised to find herself in hell, she insists that

she should be in heaven because she has confessed her sins; but Don
Juan catches her up by reminding her that confessing too many sins
"is perhaps as bad as confessing too little" . . . . In the Salvation
Army, however, there is no Juan to catch Snobby at his game. Thus
he successfully fools Jenny Hill with his exaggerated confession and
his unctuous insistence that he has "the peace that passeth hall han-
nerstennin" (p. 370). Even the experienced and worldly Mrs. Baines is
moved by his apparent conversion, and there is no indication at the
end of the play that anyone except Barbara, who has seen Snobby
steal Bill Walker's sovereign, is any the wiser. Through his presentation of Snobby and Rummy, Shaw is able to indicate his intense dissatisfaction with any religion that has as one of its basic tenets a belief
in salvation through the expiatory rite of confession.

Barbara's handling of Bill Walker, on the other hand, proceeds in
an entirely different manner. A Salvationist of the Old Testament
school, Bill has come to the Army shelter to retrieve his girl, Mog
Habbijam. Encountering resistance from Rummy Mitchens and Jenny
Hill, he strikes them both in the face. The blow to Rummy gives his
conscience no trouble, because she returns his spite with spite. "I'd
ave the lor of you, you flat eared pignosed potwalloper, if she'd let
me" . . . , she says, thereby canceling out whatever obligation Bill
might feel to regret striking her. With Jenny's absence of malice, however, Bill has had no experience. His conscience begins to bother him,
and to purge it he decides to go to Canning Town to be punished
by Todger Fairmile, Mog's new "bloke":

> Aw'm gowin to Kennintahn, to spit in Todger Fairmawl's eye. Aw
> beshed Jenny Ill's fice; an nar Aw'll git me aown fice beshed and cam
> beck an shaow it to er. Ee'll it me ardern Aw itt er. Thatll mike us
> square (p. 383).

Barbara cautions him, "Two black eyes wont make one white one,
Bill" (p. 383), but he will have nothing to do with her advice. Like
Blanco Posnet immediately after his confrontation with the woman
and child, Bill is in the throes of confusion. Upset by the voice of
God, he tries desperately to stick to his old ways, but God will not be
denied so easily. Neither Todger Fairmile nor Barbara will permit
Bill to quiet his conscience by exercising his "eye for an eye" ethic.
After his failure at Canning Town, Bill returns to the shelter and
tries one last gambit, atoning for his sin by offering the Army a
donation:

> *Bill.* It's this Christian gime o yours that Aw wownt ev played agen me:
> this blomin forgivin an neggin an jawrin that mikes a menn thet sore
> that iz lawf's a burdn to im. A wownt ev it, Aw tell you; sao tike your
> manney and stop thraowin your silly beshed fice hap agen me.

Jenny. Major: may I take a little of it for the Army?

Barbara. No: the Army is not to be bought. We want your soul, Bill; and we'll take nothing else (pp. 394–95).

Bill here is on the verge of succumbing to Barbara's method. She has first of all negated his blow-for-blow morality by accepting his deed without malice and then prevented him from purging his conscience by refusing him any artificial kind of atonement. His only recourse is to obey the voice of his conscience by becoming a new man. But Barbara has reckoned without Sir Horace Bodger and her father.

Undershaft certainly appears to be the villain of the play when he gives his check to Mrs. Baines with the deliberate purpose of forcing Barbara to lose the soul of Bill Walker and her faith in the Salvation Army. It is obvious from the first that he has become attached to his daughter. Seeing something of himself in her candor and vitality, he decides that he wants to win her to his view of life. Recognizing and respecting her genuine religious idealism he admits to Cusins, "Religion is our business at present, because it is through religion alone that we can win Barbara" (p. 286). At this point in the play (the middle of Act II) neither Cusins nor the audience is too pleased at the prospect of Barbara's being won over to Undershaft's gospel of "money and gunpowder," particularly when he discloses the means he has chosen for his conquest:

> *Cusins.* Well, I can only say that if you think you will get her away from the Salvation Army by talking to her as you have been talking to me, you dont know Barbara.
>
> *Undershaft.* My friend: I never ask for what I can buy.
>
> *Cusins (in a white fury).* Do I understand you to imply that you can buy Barbara?
>
> *Undershaft.* No; but I can buy the Salvation Army (p. 389).

He knows he can buy the Army, because he realizes that the Army cannot afford to practice Barbara's idealism. To Undershaft the basic fact about existence is that nothing can be done without money. Barbara can reject the sovereign of Bill Walker and whatever money Undershaft might offer on the grounds that she will not accept conscience money, no matter what the amount. Mrs. Baines, however, has no qualms about accepting the generous donations of Bodger and Undershaft. She may justify the acceptance of Bodger's five thousand pounds on the grounds that "heaven has found the way to make a good use of his money" (p. 399); but Shaw's juxtaposition of this incident with Barbara's refusal of Bill's sovereign makes it clear that on Christian grounds her justification is not valid. As long as the Bodgers of this world can go on buying their salvation with large donations to charity, then neither the Salvation Army nor any other religious organization that caters to them can claim to be genuinely interested in helping the lower classes. Even Snobby Price realizes this. "It combs our air and makes us good little blokes to be robbed and put upon" (p. 369), he says, to be echoed by Bill Walker's vicious "Wot prawce selvytion nah" (p. 403) at the end of the act. The irony of Bill's remark is that it should be directed at Barbara, the only member of the Army who does not deserve his reproach. She alone recognizes the ethical incongruity of the Army's decision to accept the money; and, stung by Bill's remark, she realizes that her Christianity is not that of her colleagues. Her faith is shattered, and as the others march off to give thanks for what they have received, she cries out in her agony, "Drunkenness and Murder! My God: why hast thou forsaken me?" (p. 403). This is a moment of great emotional impact in the theatre. Despite the fact that Barbara's use of Christ's words from the Cross is bound to cause some discomfort among the spectators, that very discomfort helps to heighten their awareness of the depth of Barbara's despair. Even in 1905, when most of the critics found Shaw's use of these words blasphemous and indecent, one sensitive critic could write:

> It is a very honest and daring attempt to present the agony of a devout soul when the foundations of belief disappear. It is a play of a soul's tragedy—a theatrical adaptation of the most sacred of all themes. Since I saw the Passion Play at Oberammergau I have not seen any play which represented so vividly the pathos of Gethsemane, the tragedy of Calvary.[5]

Though Barbara is the center of interest in the second act, there is much more to the act than a depiction of her faith and eventual disillusionment. In fairness to Shaw it must be said that the roles of Undershaft and Cusins are often overlooked or misinterpreted because of the sympathy which has been aroused for Barbara. Undershaft is not the sort of man who is willing to destroy Barbara's faith merely because he wants to win her to his way of life; nor are his actions designed primarily as an attack on the integrity of the Salvation Army. When questioned by Lomax in the first act as to the moral nature of the cannon business, he refuses to excuse his trade on conventional grounds:

> I am not one of those men who keep their morals and their business in water-tight compartments. All the spare money my trade rivals spend on hospitals, cathedrals, and other receptacles for conscience money, I

[5] W. T. Stead, "Impressions of the Theatre, XIV. Mr. Bernard Shaw's 'Major Barbara,'" *The Review of Reviews*, ed. W. T. Stead (London), January, 1906, p. 37.

devote to experiments and researches in improved methods of destroy-
ing life and property. I have always done so; and I always will. Therefore
your Christmas card moralities of peace on earth and goodwill among
men are of no use to me. . . . My morality—my religion—must have a
place for cannons and torpedoes in it (p. 361).

Undershaft's profession has been the source of much critical dis-
agreement, and even Shaw's most ardent admirers have been puzzled
by this character. Why should an author whose avowed purpose is to
expand man's capacity for creativity make his hero a dealer in death
and destruction? Why should a professed socialist extol a capitalist
millionaire? These are not insoluble questions, and for a hint as to
what Shaw intends us to think about Undershaft, we may turn to the
closing lines of the Preface:

> This play of mine, Major Barbara, is, I hope, both true and inspired,
> but whoever says that it all happened, and that faith in it and under-
> standing of it consists in believing that it is a record of an actual occur-
> rence, is, to speak according to Scripture, a fool and a liar, and is hereby
> solemnly denounced and cursed as such by me, the author, to all
> posterity (p. 339).

This is a warning against critical literal-mindedness. Undershaft is
a maker of cannons because gunpowder represents power over others;
he is a millionaire because money represents freedom. All of Shaw's
heroes are endowed with honesty and clarity of mind; when they take
a philosophical position they know why they have done so and are
quick to explain their reasoning to others. "Yes, money and gunpowder. Freedom and power. Command of life and command of
death" (p. 388), says Undershaft to Cusins, when asked to define his
religious creed. He is not merely playing tricks with religious terminology but expressing his belief that a man's religious faith must
be consistent, first, with his normal practices and, second, with the
amelioration of man's physical state. Cusins, naturally, is disturbed by
the lack of ordinary ethical values in Undershaft's creed, but the millionaire has a place for these:

> *Cusins.* Excuse me: is there any place in your religion for honor, justice,
>   truth, love, mercy and so forth?
> *Undershaft.* Yes: they are the graces and luxuries of a rich, strong, and
>   safe life.
> *Cusins.* Suppose one is forced to choose between them and money or
>   gunpowder?
> *Undershaft.* Choose money and gunpowder; for without enough of both
>   you cannot afford the others (p. 385).

Undershaft's attitude toward the Salvation Army may now be more clearly ascertained. From the point of view of his ethic the Army is wrong on two major counts. First, it defeats its own ends by bribing the poor with bread and dreams so that they will remain content with their lot. Since it relies on the donations of the rich for its survival, it is unwittingly on the side of the wealthy though committed to the aid of the poor. Second, through its ethic of humility it acts as an enemy to progress. As long as the mass of men believe, like Peter Shirley, that the rich are evil and the poor are good, poverty will never be eradicated:

> *Barbara.* . . . Youre not a Millionaire, are you, Peter?
> *Shirley.* No: and proud of it.
> *Undershaft (gravely).* Poverty, my friend, is not a thing to be proud of.
> *Shirley (angrily).* Who made your millions for you? Me and my like. Whats kep us poor? Keepin you rich. I wouldnt have your conscience, not for all your income.
> *Undershaft.* I wouldn't have your income, not for all your conscience, Mr Shirley (p. 330).

Shirley cannot understand that his own morality, not Undershaft, is keeping him poor. As Undershaft says later in the play, "*I* was an east ender. I moralized and starved until one day I swore that I would be a full-fed free man at all cost. . . ." (p. 435)

A religious ethic must justify itself by its tangible results, and the ethic of humility, as Undershaft demonstrates in Act II, cannot. The question of Act III is whether the munitions-making millionaire can justify his own ethic, the gospel of money and gunpowder. His course of defense is both simple and persuasive: no system which allows poverty to remain alive is acceptable, but cleanliness and respectability justify themselves. Having shown the reader the miserable conditions of London's East End and the beautiful workshops and model homes of Perivale St. Andrews,* Shaw then allows Undershaft to deliver his well-known rhetorical denunciation of poverty. In its context the speech is exceptionally powerful, and one must conclude, even in 1965, that Undershaft's position is convincing as economics. Whether it is also convincing as religion is a more difficult problem.

In Act II Barbara says, after returning to the Shelter from a street-corner meeting, "I cant talk religion to a man with bodily hunger in

---

* The most powerful argument for Undershaft's position is, of course, the town itself. In rewriting the play for the screen Shaw was able to make his millionaire even more impressive by having the family's tour of Perivale St. Andrews shown on the screen. For the additions Shaw made to the script in this section see *Major Barbara: A Screen Version* (Baltimore: Penguin Books, 1951), pp. 126–139.

his eyes" (p. 392). It is from this point that Undershaft proceeds in Act III. He respects her idealism but feels that it is misdirected, and so he goes about to rebuild her spirit by altering her ideas about the relation between physical well-being and spiritual salvation. For Barbara the primary business of life is soul-saving; that men may be hungry is a troublesome fact of secondary importance. Undershaft too is interested in souls; but soul-saving for him means something quite different. Referring to his workmen at Perivale St. Andrews he tells Barbara, "I save their souls just as I saved yours."

> *Barbara (revolted).* You saved my soul! What do you mean?
> *Undershaft.* I fed you and clothed you and housed you. I took care that you should have money enough to live handsomely—more than enough; so that you could be wasteful, careless, generous. That saved your soul from the seven deadly sins.
> *Barbara (bewildered).* The seven deadly sins!
> *Undershaft.* Yes, the deadly seven. Food, clothing, firing, rent, taxes, respectability, and children. Nothing can lift those seven millstones from Man's neck but money; and the spirit cannot soar until the millstones are lifted (pp. 433–34).

Here is the heart of Undershaft's religion: morality depends on environment. A man who does not know where his next meal is coming from will not be concerned with spiritual salvation.

Shaw's insistence through Undershaft that economic security must precede morality, that the body must be fed before the soul can contemplate higher things, has had a particularly strong influence on the work of Bertolt Brecht. The theme recurs throughout Brecht's work, particularly in *The Threepenny Opera* and in *Saint Joan of the Stockyards*. Macheath in the second act finale of the former play sings:

[Here follows the speech from *The Threepenny Opera,* ed. Eric Bentley (New York: Grove Press, 1964), pp. 66–67.—Ed.]

In Brecht's *Saint Joan of the Stockyards,* Joan Dark, the central character, is a composite of three Shavian characters, Barbara, Undershaft, and Saint Joan. Despite her name and her sex, she is, after her awakening, more like Undershaft than the other two. After having been shown the so-called "wickedness of the poor" by the Chicago meat barons, she concludes that she has seen not the wickedness of the poor but "the poverty of the poor":

> Naturally, if a man has to smash his neighbor's head for a ham sandwich so that he can satisfy his elementary needs, brother striving with brother

for the bare necessities of life, how can the sense of higher things help being stifled in the human heart? . . . Gentlemen, there is such a thing as moral purchasing-power. Raise moral purchasing-power, and there's your morality.*

Brecht's rogues and stockyard workers have no choice but to compromise their ideals for the sake of life's basic necessities; likewise, a Snobby Price or a Rummy Mitchens will be only too glad to play the game of salvation if it means getting fed.

"It is cheap work converting starving men with a Bible in one hand and a slice of bread in the other," Undershaft tells Barbara. "I will undertake to convert West Ham to Mahometanism on the same terms" (p. 435). The accusation of bribery, not Undershaft's denunciation of poverty, forces Barbara to resume her vocation as a saver of souls. Her career in the Salvation Army, she ultimately realizes, was only a vain attempt to escape from the realities of life into a "paradise of enthusiasm and prayer and soul saving" . . . . The power that Undershaft and Lazarus wield, the power of Bodger the whiskey king, is a power that permeates all of life. It is an inescapable fact of life which must be utilized if God's work is to be properly done:

> My father shall never throw it in my teeth again that my converts were bribed with bread. I have got rid of the bribe of bread. I have got rid of the bribe of heaven. Let God's work be done for its own sake: the work he had to create us to do because it cannot be done except by living men and women (p. 444).

Barbara's acceptance of Undershaft's offer has been severely criticized both as theatre and as theology. Stead, who so admired the second act, called Act III "an after-climax, and singularly unconvincing at that," [6] and Chesterton felt that "the whole point of the play is that the religious element is defeated." [7] These reactions stem in part from the failure of the critics to respond to Shaw's experimental

---

* *Seven Plays by Bertolt Brecht,* ed. Eric Bentley (New York: Grove Press, 1961), p. 186. Brecht, who borrowed material from other writers quite frequently, relied heavily on *Major Barbara* in the writing of *Saint Joan of the Stockyards.* Like Barbara, Joan Dark is a member of a Salvation Army-type group known as the Black Straw Hats. She becomes disillusioned with the impractical spirituality of the group and begins preaching something similar to the gospel of Andrew Undershaft, but at the end of the play she is defeated because she has no power to put her ideals into practice. Her "canonization" recalls the epilogue of *Saint Joan* in which her antagonists make her a saint in order to avoid the real implications of her message.

[6] *The Review of Reviews,* January, 1906, p. 40.

[7] G. K. Chesterton, *George Bernard Shaw* (New York: Hill & Wang Dramabooks, 1956), p. 145.

dramatic techniques in Act III. The highly realistic second act has always been praised, but when a reader accustomed to this sort of stage practice has to confront the futuristic and intellectualized third act he is bewildered. Barbara's loss of faith may be emotionally appreciated; her return to the colors must be intellectually understood, a difficult task for the theatregoer. The Brechtian principle of estrangement operates throughout the act, demanding that the audience put away its emotions and either follow the argument or miss the point altogether.

The real point of the ending of *Major Barbara* is that the religious element is not defeated, and through the character of Cusins, Shaw permits us to perceive this fact. The role of Adolphus Cusins is a difficult one to assess. During the first act he is quiet, taking little part in either the conversation between Barbara and her father or the affairs of the Wilton Crescent set. In the second act he is primarily a foil to Undershaft, asking the questions which will bring out the religious and economic views of the millionaire and defending the Salvation Army against Undershaft's attacks. In the third act his role suddenly assumes greater importance when it appears that he is qualified because of a legal technicality to become the next Andrew Undershaft. Cusins, whose general humanistic position has been made clear both by his profession and by his earlier actions, is willing to take over the factory if Undershaft will allow him to sell cannons to whom he pleases. Cusins obviously wants to bring his humanistic values into his new position, but for every principle he evokes, Undershaft has a refutation. Up until the last it appears that Cusins must either reject the position or accept it on Undershaft's terms, but all at once, after he has been left alone with Barbara to make his decision, his perplexities vanish. He realizes that he can become a maker of cannons without compromising his own ideals:

> *Cusins.* I want to make power for the world.
> *Barbara.* I want to make power for the world too; but it must be spiritual power.
> *Cusins.* I think all power is spiritual: these cannons will not go off by themselves. I have tried to make spiritual power by teaching Greek. But the world can never be really touched by a dead civilization. The people must have power; and the people cannot have Greek. Now the power that is made here can be wielded by all men. . . . I want a power simple enough for common men to use, yet strong enough to force the intellectual oligarchy to use its genius for the general good (p. 442).

What does all this mean? On the literal level it means nothing; Shaw is not interested in what Cusins is going to do with the cannon

business. In more general terms the power to which Cusins is referring
is Socialism. He realizes that the power which the business represents
actually runs the world despite all the work of the intellectuals and
idealists like Barbara and himself. The solution to the problem of
the evil use of power is not the idealistic opposition to it but the
distribution of it among all men through Socialism. On the purely
abstract level the final decision of Cusins and Barbara indicates that
the practical materialism of Undershaft is not Shaw's final solution
to the spiritual dilemma of mankind. Even Undershaft himself realizes
this. Before his departure he cautions Cusins, "Plato says, my friend,
that society cannot be saved until either the Professors of Greek take
to making gunpowder, or else the makers of gunpowder become
Professors of Greek" (p. 439). The reference to Plato's *Republic* implies that the salvation of society can be achieved only through a
union of spiritual wisdom (Barbara), intellectual wisdom (Cusins),
and material power (Undershaft). Eric Bentley expresses the same
thought when he states that Cusins is designed to represent "the
synthesis of Barbara's idealism and her father's realism." [8]

All this is consistent with Shaw's usual practice. The world of *The
Devil's Disciple* is saved through a union of Dick's spirituality and
Anderson's practicality, and the world of *John Bull's Other Island*,
written just before *Major Barbara*, is not saved because Doyle, Broadbent, and Keegan are temperamentally unable to merge their forces.
The trouble with *Major Barbara* is that the idea of a union comes
too late. Bentley suggests that Shaw's decision to have Cusins represent
a higher kind of morality was an afterthought; perhaps the entire
last scene between Cusins and Barbara was an afterthought. The
possibility exists that Shaw wrote the scene because he realized that
he had carried his support of Undershaft's position further than he
had really desired. At the end the real victory is Undershaft's, though
Shaw did not intend it.

For all this *Major Barbara* is still on the side of the religious. In
1929 Reinhold Niebuhr wrote: "If it is dangerous to entertain great
moral ideals without attempting to realize them in life, it is even more
perilous to proclaim them in abstract terms without bringing them
into juxtaposition with the specific social and moral issues of the
day." [9] This is the challenge that Undershaft offers to Barbara and
Cusins, and their response to that challenge is a genuinely religious
one. They have learned that moral ideals cannot be realized through
otherworldliness and that one must utilize the power of this world,

[8] Eric Bentley, *Bernard Shaw*, amended ed. (New York: New Directions, 1957),
p. 167.
[9] Reinhold Niebuhr, *Leaves from the Notebooks of a Tamed Cynic* (New York:
Living Age Books, 1957), pp. 15–16.

not oppose it. The optimism of Barbara and Cusins is justified, because they understand that the victory of Undershaft does not imply defeat for the higher morality which they represent; his triumph is but a necessary prelude to theirs.

The Undershaft Maxims

by Bernard Dukore

In the third act of Bernard Shaw's *Major Barbara*, Andrew Undershaft, attempting to bridge the "abyss of moral horror" which Adolphus Cusins claims lies between him and the Undershaft factory, recites the maxims of the previous Undershafts, concluding with his own. Listed separately for more convenient reference, they are:

[I] The first Undershaft wrote up in his shop IF GOD GAVE THE HAND, LET NOT MAN WITHHOLD THE SWORD.

[II] The second wrote up ALL HAVE THE RIGHT TO FIGHT: NONE HAVE THE RIGHT TO JUDGE.

[III] The third wrote up TO MAN THE WEAPON: TO HEAVEN THE VICTORY.

[IV] The fourth had no literary turn; so he did not write up anything; but he sold cannons to Napoleon under the nose of George the Third.

[V] The fifth wrote up PEACE SHALL NOT PREVAIL SAVE WITH A SWORD IN HER HAND.

[VI] The sixth, my master, was the best of all. He wrote up NOTHING IS EVER DONE IN THIS WORLD UNTIL MEN ARE PREPARED TO KILL ONE ANOTHER IF IT IS NOT DONE.

[VII] After that, there was nothing left for the seventh to say. So he wrote up, simply, UNASHAMED.

Since Undershaft is attempting to convert Cusins and Barbara to his doctrine of realism and power, and since these six maxims and one non-maxim are means to this end, it is remarkable that they have received virtually no attention. In this essay, I will try to demonstrate that these seven principles are not only summaries of the various arguments used by Undershaft in the process of converting Cusins, but also that they are the bases of Cusins' attempt to justify his decision to Barbara. In addition, I would like to suggest what his slogan might be when he becomes the eighth Andrew Undershaft.

The motto of the present Andrew Undershaft (Andrew Undershaft VII) is one of the first things we learn about him. Early in the

"The Undershaft Maxims" by Bernard Dukore. From Modern Drama, *IX (May, 1966), 90–100. Reprinted by permission of* Modern Drama.

expository dialogue between Lady Britomart and Stephen, she complains to her son that since her husband's motto was "Unashamed," everyone knew that his parents were unmarried. This lack of shame is soon evident after Undershaft's arrival when he calls himself "a profiteer in mutilation and murder," confesses that he is in an especially amiable humor because that morning a weapon of his that had formerly destroyed thirteen dummy soldiers managed to demolish twenty-seven, and refuses to be hypocritical when Lomax suggests that "the more destructive war becomes, the sooner it will be abolished." "Not at all," Undershaft candidly replies.

> The more destructive war becomes the more fascinating we find it. No, Mr. Lomax: I am obliged to you for making the usual excuse for my trade; but I am not ashamed of it. I am not one of those men who keep their morals and their business in water-tight compartments. All the spare money my trade rivals spend on hospitals, cathedrals, and other receptacles for conscience money, I devote to experiments and researches in improved methods of destroying life and property. I have always done so; and I always shall. Therefore your Christmas card moralities of peace on earth and goodwill among men are of no use to me. Your Christianity, which enjoins you to resist not evil, and to turn the other cheek, would make me a bankrupt. My morality—my religion—must have a place for cannons and torpedoes in it.

Also in the first act, Undershaft has dialogue that anticipates the first and third slogans, which link guns and God:

> *Undershaft.* . . . I am rather interested in the Salvation Army. Its motto might be my own: Blood and Fire.
> *Lomax (shocked).* But not your sort of blood and fire, you know.
> *Undershaft.* My sort of blood cleanses: my sort of fire purifies.

However, neither of these speeches is addressed to Cusins. Indeed, the Greek professor is a comparatively minor figure in the first act. Although his abilities are suggested when he humbugs Lady Britomart and Lomax, when he takes charge of the introductions in order to clarify social relationships for the long-absent head of the household, and when he explains a moral precept to the confused Lomax, he is in the first act little more than an observer. In the second act he becomes Undershaft's confederate, and it is not until the third act that he engages in a major battle with his future father-in-law. Therefore, it is in the final two acts, especially the third, when Undershaft attempts to win Cusins first as an accomplice and then as a successor, that we find Undershaft consistently employing arguments and giving demonstrations which exemplify the seven principles of the seven Undershafts.

[I] The first principle, which implies that weapons are part of the divine plan, is suggested in the second act when Undershaft tells Cusins that two things are necessary to salvation: "Money and gunpowder." Shortly thereafter, he explains that money and gunpowder mean "Freedom and power. Command of life and command of death."

[II] The second maxim lies behind what Undershaft calls "the true faith of an Armorer," which he defines in the third act:

> To give arms to all men who offer an honest price for them, without respect of persons or principles: to aristocrat and republican, to Nihilist and Tsar, to Capitalist and Socialist, to Protestant and Catholic, to burglar and policeman, to black man, white man and yellow man, to all sorts and conditions, all nationalities, all faiths, all follies, all causes and all crimes.

Under the terms of the Armorer's faith, Undershaft is obligated to "take an order from a good man as cheerfully as from a bad one." In reversing the traditional pattern of the phrase (that he would be obligated to take an order from a *bad* man as cheerfully as from a *good* one), he not only implicitly accepts the diabolonian labels which Cusins heaps upon him but also uses the diabolonian concept to emphasize to Cusins that the power he manufactures does not have a label of "moral" or "immoral" attached to it.

[III] The wielder of power is but a holder of power, not an owner of power. Cusins had recognized this precept in the second act when he referred to "The power Barbara wields here—the power that wields Barbara herself. . . ." Undershaft admits that this principle applies to himself as well, that he does not drive the munitions factory but is driven by it; what does drive it, he asserts, is "A will of which I am a part." When Cusins objects that the factory is driven not by a metaphysical will but "by the most rascally part of society, the money hunters, the pleasure hunters, the military promotions hunters," Undershaft counters with the reminders that the rascals are in control only when the good people do not fight them, and that his weapons are for sale to either. The weapons are there for man to use: their use and the result of that use are part of the continual struggle of the Life Force in its movement upward.

[IV] Although Andrew Undershaft VII tells us that Andrew Undershaft IV wrote no maxim upon the wall, he also tells us that he sold weapons to Napoleon under George III's nose. Instead of talking, the fourth Andrew Undershaft did things. Effective actions render discussion meaningless. As Shaw later said, "Logic is futile in the face of the accomplished fact"; it is useless to "argue with an earthquake." [1]

---

[1] Quoted in Archibald Henderson, *George Bernard Shaw: Man of the Century* (New York, 1956), p. 344. This statement was made in reference to the Russian Revolution.

Some of Undershaft's most effective "arguments" take the form of demonstrations. In the second act, for example, Undershaft tells Cusins that the Salvation Army—"the Church of the poor," as the latter calls it—actually helps *him*. When Cusins protests that the Army makes the poor sober, attached to their homes, happy, and unselfish, and that it turns their thoughts to heavenly things, Undershaft interprets this in a manner which demonstrates that these "virtues" operate to his advantage: sober workers create larger profits, if they are attached to their homes "they will put up with anything sooner than change their shop," happy workers are "An invaluable safeguard against revolution," unselfish means "Indifferent to their own interests," and if their thoughts are on heavenly things these thoughts are not then on Trade Unionism or Socialism. At this point, as if to provide a living example of the validity of Undershaft's interpretation, Peter Shirley enters. "And this," announces Undershaft as he refers to the new arrival, "is an honest man!" Shirley underscores Undershaft's argument: "Yes; and what av I got by it?" Undershaft's reply is as much to Cusins as to Shirley: "Oh, your employers must have a good deal by it from first to last." Cusins, as though indicating his acceptance of Undershaft's interpretation, sits beside him, *"overwhelmed."* Later in the second act, Undershaft demonstrates his power by "buying" the Salvation Army. He does not present verbal arguments on whether he can do it: he simply does it. Mrs. Bains' rhetorical question—"Barbara: will there be less drinking or more if all those poor souls we are saving come tomorrow and find the doors of our shelters shut in their faces?"—is reminiscent of General Booth's statement that he would take money from the Devil himself to further the work of the Army. However, her remark is undercut by her next line, "Lord Saxmundham gives us the money to stop drinking—to take his own business from him." Undershaft further undermines her position when he states, as he hands her his check, "I give you this money to help you to hasten my own commercial ruin." Cusins, who a few minutes previously had been persuaded that the Salvation Army helps Undershaft realize greater profits, perceives the deviltry and announces, *"in an ecstacy of mischief,"* that the millennium will be inaugurated by such unselfishness. Cusins understands that by making the Army dependent upon them for its source of income, Bodger and Undershaft can cut off that source if ever the Army becomes effective. He sees, too, that the Army helps Bodger and Undershaft thrive because it does not attack causes but merely attempts to alleviate some of the results, while at the same time giving the illusion that basic measures are being undertaken. As Desmond MacCarthy stated, the Army tends "to keep the poor quiet, by making them less discontented with conditions which they ought to die rather than stand,

and the rich . . . thinking they are just and honest, by offering them opportunities of being generous and kind; in short, . . . [it keeps] those who should be indignant, servile, and those who ought to be uneasy, self-satisfied." [2] Undershaft's method of arguing by effective action is emphasized when he joins the Salvation Army parade shouting " 'My ducats and my daughter'!" The quotation is from *The Merchant of Venice*, and is spoken by Shylock when he learns that his daughter has run away from home and taken his money. Undershaft is ironic, for he has donated his money to "buy" his daughter's home in order to make her leave it for his. Shylock loses his money as he loses his daughter; Undershaft invests his money to regain his daughter.

The pragmatic principle of Andrew Undershaft IV is repeated several times by Andrew Undershaft VII in the third act. When your religion does not fit the facts, he advises, scrap it and get one that does. When asked to justify cleanliness and respectability he replies that they "do not need justification . . . they justify themselves." And he invites Barbara to bring the "half-saved" Bill Walker to him at Perivale St. Andrews: "I will drag his soul back again to salvation for you. Not by words and dreams; but by thirty-eight shillings a week, a sound house in a handsome street, and a permanent job."

[V] When Cusins says that he hates war, Undershaft defines hatred as "the coward's revenge for being intimidated" and directly challenges him to seize the sword in order to make peace prevail: "Dare you make war on war? Here are the means. . . .'"

[VI] Undershaft recounts that it was only when he acted on the principle that nothing is ever accomplished until one is ready to kill if it is not accomplished, that he was able to rise from poverty: "I moralized and starved until one day I swore that I would be a full-fed free man at all costs; that *nothing should stop me except a bullet, neither reason nor morals nor the lives of other men*. I said 'Thou shalt starve ere I starve'; and with that word I became free and great." [3] This principle is also behind his assertion, "Poverty and

[2] Desmond MacCarthy, *Shaw* (London, 1951), p. 47.

[3] My italics. Although the speech is thoroughly appropriate to this ex-poverty-stricken millionaire, we should not accept it as self-evidently true. As Desmond MacCarthy very sensibly pointed out, Undershaft "talks very big about having been prepared to kill anybody as long as he was poor; but what did he *do*? Did he found his fortunes by knocking an old woman on the head and stealing her watch, or by going into partnership with a Mrs. Warren? No, of course not; he stuck to his desk like a good young man, inched and pinched until he had made himself useful to the firm, and then took good care not to be put upon." (*Ibid.*, p. 48). MacCarthy's substitute biography may not be completely acceptable, but his point—that Undershaft's description of his rise is not accurate—is well taken.

slavery have stood up for centuries to your sermons and leading articles: they will not stand up to my machine guns" and his challenge, "Dont preach at them: dont reason with them. Kill them." Elections accomplish nothing, for voting merely changes the names of the cabinet members; killing, on the other hand, "is the final test of conviction, the only lever strong enough to overturn a social system, the only way of saying Must." He presses the point to Cusins: "Whatever can blow men up can blow society up. The history of the world is the history of those who had courage enough to embrace this truth." And he drives it home with an audacious appeal to an authority from Cusins' camp: "Plato says, my friend, that society cannot be saved until either the Professors of Greek take to making gunpowder, or else the makers of gunpowder become Professors of Greek."

[VII] In a sense, "Unashamed" underlies all of the others. An attitude of realism pervades Undershaft's actions and deeds. He sees things as they are and labels them for what they are.

> *Lady Britomart.* . . . And you, Adolphus, ought to know better than to go about saying that wrong things are true. What does it matter whether they are true if they are wrong?
>
> *Undershaft.* What does it matter whether they are wrong if they are true?

Undershaft refuses to hide behind moralistic labels. ("He never does a proper thing without giving an improper reason for it," Lady Britomart complains to Cusins.) When such labels prevent Cusins from seeing the necessity for seizing the power which Undershaft offers him, the latter is quick to point this out to him. Cusins suggests Pity as a concept he must reckon with, and Undershaft promptly defines it as "The scavenger of misery." Cusins next suggests Love, and Undershaft reveals the absurdity of such a concept: "You love the needy and the outcast: you love the oppressed races, the negro, the Indian ryot, the underdog everywhere. Do you love the Japanese? Do you love the French? Do you love the English?" (In other words, if you love the oppressed, how can you at the same time love the oppressors?) Finally, Cusins himself rejects Forgiveness as "a beggar's refuge" and agrees with Undershaft that "we must pay our debts."

The precepts of the seven Andrew Undershafts embody the principles behind the arguments given and the actions taken by the present Undershaft. These arguments and actions convince Cusins that he should accept the offer to become Andrew Undershaft VIII.

Moreover, these principles are behind Cusins' attempt to prove to Barbara that he is right to accept this offer. When the two are left alone to discuss the matter, Cusins immediately announces that he is going to accept Undershaft's offer,[4] and then attempts to justify his decision to her. His efforts to convince *her* are governed by the same principles as Undershaft's attempts to persuade *him*. In fact, Cusins' arguments in this final scene recapitulate, almost in sequence, the separate stages in the Undershaft progression as he goes through what are in effect variations of the doctrines of the seven Undershafts.

[I] Cusins tells Barbara that what he is now agreeing to accept is not a trifle but the sword—"neither money nor position nor comfort, but . . . reality and . . . power."

[II] See final section below.

[III] He realizes that he will be an agent for a power greater than himself, and that he will make power not for himself but for the world. He perceives that although this power, whatever it may be, must be in the form of a weapon capable of being used by man, it is ultimately a spiritual power. "I think all power is spiritual," he says; "these cannons will not go off by themselves."

[IV] The principle of effective action rather than fine words is behind Cusins' recollection of his having given a gun and ammunition, instead of a copy of Plato's *Republic*, to a pupil who went off to fight for Greece against Turkey. He accepts both the moral responsibilty and the implications of this deed: "The blood of every Turk he shot —if he shot any—is on my head as well as on Undershaft's. That act committed me to this place for ever."

[V] Cusins understands that in order for a morality to prevail, man must control the means to enforce it.

Barbara. Is there no higher power than that *(Pointing to the shell)*?

Cusins. Yes; but that power can destroy the higher powers just as a tiger can destroy a man: therefore Man must master that power first.

[VI] He realizes that only if one is prepared to go to the extreme, be willing to kill, will genuine progress be made: "Your father's challenge has beaten me. Dare I make war on war? I dare. I must. I will."

[VII] Previously, traditional attitudes implied by such words as "Pity" and "Love" bothered Cusins. Now, he is "Unashamed." A realistic outlook prevails as he himself defines the meaning of his deeds. When Barbara accuses him of selling his soul for the inheritance

---

[4] Cusins has not until this point announced his decision. Although Stephen assumes that he has not yet arrived at a decision ("Think before you decide," he advises), Undershaft evidently has no doubt but that Cusins will accept. His parting words to Cusins are, "Come when you please: before a week you will come at six and stay until I turn you out for the sake of your health" and his first words to Cusins upon his return from the gun cotton shed are not "What is your decision?" but "Well? What does *she* say?" (My italics.)

he is not troubled by the phrase, but uses that very phrase as part of his justification for his action:

> It is not the sale of my soul that troubles me: I have sold it too often to care about that. I have sold it for a professorship. I have sold it for an income. I have sold it to escape being imprisoned for refusing to pay taxes for hangman's ropes and unjust wars and things that I abhor. What is all human conduct but the daily and hourly sale of our souls for trifles? What I am now selling it for is neither money nor position nor comfort, but for reality and for power.

He realizes that these are necessary means to his ends. Unashamed of his decision, he announces it even at the risk of losing her. He begins his explanation with "You understand, don't you, that I had to decide without consulting you" and concludes it with "And now, is it all over between us?"

"My good Machiavelli," says Cusins to Undershaft after the latter has recited the family slogans, "I shall certainly write something up on the wall; only, as I shall write it in Greek, you won't be able to read it." Although we are not told what Cusins will write, we are given several hints.

Chief among these is the conspicuous absence in his final scene with Barbara of a paraphrase of the second Undershaft maxim, which is itself an aphoristic paraphrase of the Armorer's faith. Actually, Cusins had explicitly repudiated this principle: "But as to your Armorer's faith, if I take my neck out of the noose of my own morality I am not going to put it into the noose of yours. I shall sell cannons to whom I please and refuse them to whom I please. So there!" Although Undershaft replies that from the moment Cusins succeeds to the inheritance he will never again do as he pleases, we have only Undershaft's word that this will be the case. What will happen in the future is an open question.

In the present, we see Cusins engaging in several battles with Undershaft, and winning three and possibly four of them. First, he convinces Undershaft to accept him as a *bona fide* bastard. Second, he persuades him that his education has had an unusual result: it has not destroyed his mind but nourished it. "Well, I cannot afford to be too particular," admits Undershaft, "you have cornered the foundling market. Let it pass. You are eligible, Euripides: you are eligible." Third, he defeats Undershaft on Undershaft's own ground, business, when he forces him to raise his salary. The fourth encounter, concerning Cusins' hours of labor, ends ambiguously. When Undershaft indicates that he expects Cusins' working day to begin at six in the morning, the younger man *"firmly"* responds, "Not on any account. I will see the whole establishment blown up with its own dynamite before I will get up at five. My hours are healthy, rational hours: eleven to five." Although Undershaft apparently acquiesces—"Come when you please"—he immediately indicates that in time he will prevail: "before a week you will come at six and stay until I turn you out for the sake of your health." Cusins' hours are not mentioned again until the final line of the play, when Undershaft says to him, "Six o'clock tomorrow morning, Euripides." Cusins, however, says nothing either in assent or in dissent. We are left with ambiguity.

Nevertheless, on the basis of Cusins' three victories and on the basis of a new principle enunciated in his final scene with Barbara— a principle which runs counter to that of the Armorer's faith and the second Undershaft maxim—we have what appears to be the foundation for a maxim for Andrew Undershaft VIII.

In the second act, Undershaft had indicated—*"with a shrug of contempt for the mob"*—his sentiments about the common man: "What have we three [himself, Cusins, and Barbara] to do with the common mob of slaves and idolators? . . . This love of the common people may please an earl's granddaughter and a university professor; but I have been a common man and a poor man; and it has no romance for me." Cusins, apparently, is not won over to this point of view, for at the end of the third act he tells Barbara what he hopes to accomplish as Andrew Undershaft VIII:

> As a teacher of Greek I gave the intellectual man weapons against the common man. I now want to give the common man weapons against the intellectual man. I love the common people. I want to arm them against the lawyers, the doctors, the priests, the literary men, the professors, the artists, and the politicians, who, once in authority, are more disastrous and tyrannical than all the fools, rascals, and impostors. *I want a power simple enough for common men to use, yet strong enough to force the intellectual oligarchy to use its genius for the general good.*[5]

This sentiment is different from any of the principles of the other Andrew Undershafts and actually contradicts the one behind the second maxim. A slogan similar to the italicized sentence may become

[5] My italics. All of the quotations I have used are from the revised version of the play which Shaw prepared for the 1931 Standard Edition of his works published in London by Constable. Subsequent English and American editions of the play are substantially the same as this one. However, when Shaw turned *Major Barbara* into a film in 1940, he revised several passages, including the one I have just cited. He altered the first two sentences of the quotation in a way which clarifies Cusins' intentions and serves as more effective preparation for the sentence I have italicized: "As a teacher of Greek I gave the rich man an intellectual weapon against the poor man. I now want to give the poor man material weapons against the intellectual man."—Bernard Shaw, *Major Barbara: A Screen Version* (Baltimore, 1957), p. 157.

the motto that the next Andrew Undershaft will write upon the wall
in his shop.

For Cusins, all do not have the right to fight, and he intends to
take upon himself the right to judge who does have that right. He
wishes to be one of the intellectual oligarchy who will run the world
and who, in running it, will give the common people the means of
seeing to it that he and those like him use their genius for the general
good rather than for the good of the wealthy. Andrew Undershaft VII
does not represent the final word in social progress. No one person
or principle, to Shaw, represents the *final* word in any sort of progress,[6]
and to think otherwise is a sign of myopia. I take this to be one of
Shaw's points when he has the seventh Undershaft say of the maxim
of the sixth, "After that, there was nothing left for the seventh to
say." On the contrary, *much* remains to be said. Indeed, it would be
odd to assume that the socialist Shaw would embrace the paternalistic
capitalism of Andrew Undershaft VII as the final word in social
evolution.[7] The social achievements of this Andrew Undershaft will
be used as a foundation upon which the next Undershaft hopes to
build. Cusins will attempt to broaden the base of power, to turn
Perivale St. Andrews from a benevolent despotism to an enlightened
—and probably socialist[8]—democracy, to give the common people
the power now wielded by their rulers.

[6] In *The Simpleton of the Unexpected Isles,* he has an angel, who has dropped
down from Heaven to announce the Judgment Day, make the statement, "An
angel is far from being the perfect organism you imagine. There is always something better."

[7] One might recall in this connection what Shaw said of Broadbent in his preface
to *John Bull's Other Island,* "Much as I like him, I object to be governed by
him. . . ."

[8] The identification of Cusins as future maker of socialism in contrast to Undershaft as present capitalist monarch is more explicit in the film version than in any
of the play versions I have examined. In addition to the change noted above,
footnote 5, there is another change which also makes much clearer the conflict
between capitalism and socialism, and at the same time implies that Cusins will
be on the side of the latter. In the play Cusins tells Barbara that Perivale St.
Andrews "is driven by the most rascally part of society, the money hunters, the
pleasure hunters, the military promotion hunters; and he is their slave." Undershaft reminds Cusins of the Armorer's faith. "I will take an order from a good man
as cheerfully as from a bad one," he says, and challenges him: "If you good people prefer preaching and shirking to buying my weapons and fighting the rascals,
don't blame me." In the motion picture version Cusins' statement is, "The place
is driven by Capitalist money hunters; and he is their slave," and Undershaft's
challenge, "If you good people prefer preaching and shirking to buying my weapons
and fighting the money hunters, dont blame me." (*Screen Version,* p. 147) The
"bad" people and "the rascals" are now identified.

Major Barbara

by Margery M. Morgan

"Without contraries is no progression."

Blake, *The Marriage of
Heaven and Hell*

Major Barbara is undoubtedly one of Shaw's finest plays: in it an
intellectual structure of considerable precision and intricacy is combined with an abundance of invention, a spontaneous energy of movement and a surprisingly subtle emotional pattern.[1] A freely flowing
subconscious creativity has enriched the play as some of his late work,
including *The Millionairess,* is not enriched, and without confusing
its clarity as *Candida* was, I think, confused. Though the break-away
from principles of dramatic organization learned from Ibsen was not
far ahead, it is not foreshadowed in *Major Barbara* even to the extent
it was in *John Bull's Other Island.* In *Major Barbara,* Shaw still
pursues his philosophical purpose by the method of dialectic: discover-
ing truth through the confrontation of opposites. His analytic approach to his subject is reflected in a number of overlapping, in-
completely synchronized conflicts. His main characters occupy well
defined philosophical positions, representing distinct approaches to
life and distinct modes of experience, whose adequacy is tested in the
course of, and as part of, the action. The mainspring of the play
seems to have been provided by Shaw's response to Blake, reinforced
by a reading of Nietzsche where he is closest to Blake. The dialectical

*"Major Barbara" by Margery M. Morgan. Copyright © 1970 by Margery M.
Morgan. This is the draft of a chapter which will appear in revised form in a
forthcoming book,* The Shavian Playground, *by Margery M. Morgan. The quotations from* The Birth of Tragedy *by Friedrich Nietzsche are translated by W. A.
Haussmann in Vol. I of* The Complete Works *of Friedrich Nietzsche, ed. Oscar
Levy [1909–1911] (New York: Russell & Russell, 1964), pp. [21]–187. Reprinted by permission of Russell & Russell and George Allen & Unwin Ltd.*

[1] The impact this play made on Brecht is indicated by the extent to which it
inspired *St. Joan of the Stockyards.*

terms of *The Marriage of Heaven and Hell* define the ironic stance
Shaw holds throughout:

> Without contraries is no progression. Attraction and repulsion, reason
> and energy, love and hate, are necessary to human existence.
>
> From these contraries spring what the religious call good and evil. Good
> is the passive that obeys reason; evil is the active springing from energy.
>
> Good is heaven. Evil is hell.

The "Voice of the Devil" issues from Andrew Undershaft, in whom
Blake's version of Satan and Nietzsche's Dionysos unite to form a
unique comic character. Certainly nowhere else in Shaw's work do
we come so close to the imaginative sense of:

1. Man has no body distinct from his soul . . .
2. Energy is the only life, and is from the body; and reason is the bound
   or outward circumference of energy,

and, above all, the sense of:

3. Energy is eternal delight.[2]

The peculiarly Shavian variety of Ibsenite dramatic structure,
imitated from the Platonic dialogue, is apparent in verbal debates on
the play's basic themes, rationally conceived and conducted to a
great extent in abstract terms. A centrally placed sub-plot, involving
the heroine herself in conflict with a character from a sub-group,
brings into focus the other areas of the play's design. The realism of
its settings—the library in Wilton Crescent, the Salvation Army shelter
in Canning Town and the especially topical Garden City[3]—establishes
it as a critique of actual society. Within the framework of an Edwardian comedy of manners, philosophical demonstration is further set
off by the thinly disguised enactment of folk-tale quests and divine
rituals.

Shaw originally thought of calling the play *Andrew Undershaft's
Profession,* which implies a reworking of the same basic themes as

---

[2] The self-evident relationship of these quotations from *The Marriage of Heaven
and Hell* to *Major Barbara* is objectively confirmed by Shaw's comment in the
Preface to *Three Plays for Puritans*: "Let those who have praised my originality
in conceiving Dick Dudgeon's strange religion read Blake's Marriage of Heaven
and Hell, and I shall be fortunate if they do not rail at me for a plagiarist." This
is the starting point of Irvine Fiske's essay, "Bernard Shaw and William Blake,"
Shavian Tract No. 2, reprinted in *G. B. Shaw: A Collection of Critical Essays,* ed.
R. J. Kaufmann, (Englewood Cliffs, N.J.: Prentice-Hall, 1965), pp. 170–78. The link
with *Major Barbara* is not noted there.

[3] The fact that Ebenezer Howard, as originator of the Garden City idea, was
an exponent of the Smiles' Self-Help attitude to the working-class, drawing the
teeth of revolt, is relevant to the interpretation of Shaw's play.

in *Mrs. Warren's Profession* (and *Widowers' Houses* before that): a confrontation of the innocence of society's dupes with the disillusion of its exploiters. The child-parent relationship of Vivie and Mrs. Warren, through which this confrontation had been presented, anticipated the relationship of Barbara to Andrew Undershaft. The plan was complicated in the process of writing when Shaw transformed Barbara's *fiancé* from a young man-about-town like Lomax (for so he is characterized at the beginning of the Derry long-hand version) to a Professor of Greek. I think we can assume that Cusins was at first envisaged as playing a minor or choric role comparable to Frank's in the earlier play: that of an observer and commentator who also sets the comic tone of the drama. In his character of observer, the Professor of Greek is qualified to identify for us the philosophical issues and the mythopoetic analogues as they arise. His intellectual quality does not entirely obscure the lineaments of the clown; but he plays the ironical fool to Lomax's "natural." As a more considerable and distinguished member of society, he is also fitted to become one of the main pivots of the dramatic scheme. The extension in the play's significance which has followed from this later conception of the character culminates in a scrap of dialogue inserted as an afterthought in the long-hand text of Act III:

Undershaft. . . . Remember the words of Plato.
Cusins (starting). Plato! You dare to quote Plato to me!
Undershaft. Plato says, my friend, that society cannot be saved until either the Professors of Greek take to making gunpowder, or else the makers of gunpowder become Professors of Greek.

To the opposition between Undershaft and Barbara there has been added an independent opposition between Undershaft and Cusins, tending towards an ultimate reconciliation. Of course, these are various examples of a single basic conflict between idealism and realism. But the placing of the two in the progress of the drama must absolve Shaw from any charge of tautology: Barbara, the indubitable protagonist of Act II, subsides into watchfulness in Act III, while Cusins takes over from her, is put to the test, and makes the crucial decision; her endorsement of this in the last moments of the play lends strength to the impression that he has indeed been deputising for her.[4] It is dramatically necessary, after her defeat by Undershaft in Act II, that the initiative should pass from Barbara. Cusins carries the play into its final movement, as he makes his pact with

[4] It is just possible that we have here an imitation of the "substitution of persons" Gilbert Murray observed in Euripides' treatment of Dionysos myths (See "Excursus on Ritual Forms in Greek Tragedy," included in Jane Harrison's *Themis*—Meridian Books edition, pp. 341–63, esp. p. 347) as we have in *Misalliance*.

Undershaft. This has the effect of restoring Barbara to her proper centrality, though now in alliance with her former opponents. Cusins' function has been to introduce the dialectical synthesis, after the sharply defined opposition between the views of father and daughter. The reconciliation he proposes between power and service, the balance of realism with idealism, corresponds, of course, to the Platonic advocacy of the philosopher-king (*Republic*, Book V);[5] it is also in the spirit of Fabian compromise and an element in the ultimately comfortable imaginative world of this play.

Undershaft, the manufacturer of armaments, represents a different quality of opposition from Sartorius, the slum landlord, or Mrs. Warren, owner-director of an international chain of brothels. Whereas those earlier creations remain prisoners of society, outcasts from respectability, and in presentation are touched with the pathos of melodrama, the nature of the commodity Undershaft traffics in, power itself, puts him in mastery over society and gives him the confidence and authority to set up his sign: "UNASHAMED." Shaw has, in *Major Barbara*, grasped the basic nature of the threat offered to the intellect by the actual world: the challenge of undifferentiated force and mass in the physical universe to the essentially sole and individual; the ruthless and mindless violence that "can destroy the higher power just as a tiger can destroy a man."

This, of course, is the power that Nietzsche called dionysiac and regarded as the antithesis of the Socratic poise he defined as apollonian.[6] "The business of the Salvation Army is to save, not to wrangle about the name of the pathfinder," declares Cusins, "Dionysos or another: what does it matter?" The protest was anticipated by Nietzsche himself in his Preface to *The Birth of Tragedy*:

It was *against* morality, therefore, that my instinct, as an intercessory instinct for life, turned in this questionable book, inventing for itself a fundamental counter-dogma and counter-valuation of life, purely artistic, purely *anti-Christian*. What should I call it? As a philologist and man of words I baptised it, not without some liberty—for who could be sure of

    [5] Did G.B.S., writing this play—and discussing it with Gilbert Murray—have also in mind Plato's discussion of trade in armaments in *Politics*, and the conclusion that this traffic, necessary for the state, ought not to be carried on by private individuals for their own profit?
    [6] Louis Crompton has taken up the point of Shaw's debt to Nietzsche and his concept of Dionysos in "Shaw's Challenge to Liberalism," reprinted in *G. B. Shaw*, ed. Kaufmann, pp. 88–99. I have let my discussion of the matter stand, as its direction is different from Mr. Crompton's. The probability of Shaw's early familiarity with Nietzsche's work, in a manuscript translation by W. A. Haussmann, and a comparison of his use of this source in *Major Barbara* with Yeats's in *The Resurrection* are themes of my article, "Shaw, Yeats, Nietzsche, and the Religion of Art," *Komos* I (English Department, Monash University, 1967), 24–34.

the proper name of the Antichrist?—with the name of a Greek god: I
called it *Dionysian*. (Trans. W. A. Haussmann, p. 11)

In fact, Dionysos is mentioned in the dialogue with sufficient fre-
quency to justify entirely the critics Shaw attacked in his Preface for
labelling his play as derivative from Nietzschean philosophy. Barbara
Undershaft, the evangelist, represents the orthodox Christian attitude
that Nietzsche was determined to oppose. Her father, whom Cusins
nicknames "Prince of Darkness" and "Mephistopheles," as well as
"Dionysos" and "Machiavelli," challenges her with the "fundamental
counter-dogma":

> Leave it to the poor to pretend that poverty is a blessing: leave it to the
> coward to make a religion of his cowardice by preaching humility;
>
> I had rather be a thief than a pauper. I had rather be a murderer than
> a slave. I don't want to be either; but if you force the alternative on me,
> then, by Heaven, I'll choose the braver and more moral one.

In adding to these two the figure of a Professor of Greek, Shaw had
supplied his play with a representative of that dispassionate and
philosophical Hellenic consciousness upon which Nietzsche saw the
originally Asiatic religion of Dionysos as having broken in, at a critical
point in the history of civilization. The passage in *The Birth of
Tragedy* that supplies the fullest account of this event and its consequences can be related illuminatingly to *Major Barbara*. It is indeed
difficult to resist the conclusion that here we have the germ from which
the whole play grew in Shaw's imagination— Nietzsche begins with
a statement of the tremendous division between the Greek worship of
Dionysos and the barbarian cults of Dionysos that preceded it. Already
this hints at the rationale of supplying Undershaft with a double
opposition in, first, the aptly named Barbara, and then Professor
Cusins. The famous essay goes on to cite evidence of the Panic lust
and cruelty widely typical of savage festivals in the ancient world and
which Nietzsche thinks of as reflected in later Witches' Sabbaths.
(*op. cit.*, pp. 29–30)
  Now Shaw has almost entirely dissociated these forces from his
principal characters. They are symbolically represented in the play
by Undershaft's explosives and the wars in which they are used: "the
men and lads torn to pieces with shrapnel and poisoned with lyddite!
. . . the oceans of blood . . . the ravaged crops!"—by "Bodger's
Whisky in letters of fire against the sky," by the drum that Cusins
beats, and by the Salvation Army motto of "Blood and Fire!" More
directly, they are present in the physical violence with which Bill

Walker disturbs the shelter, in Act II, and for which he has prepared himself by drinking gin:

> Aw'm nao gin drinker . . . ; bat when Aw want to give my girl a bloomin good awdin Aw lawk to ev a bit o devil in me.

Returning to Nietzsche, we find the immunity of Shaw's principal characters, the educated and the aristocratic, accounted for:

> For some time . . . it would seem that the Greeks were perfectly secure and guarded against the feverish agitations of these festivals . . . by the figure of Apollo himself rising here in full pride, who could not have held out the Gorgon's head to a more dangerous power than this grotesquely uncouth Dionysian. It is in Doric art that this majestically-rejecting attitude of Apollo perpetuated itself. (*op. cit.,* p. 30)

The production note which prepares for Cusins' first entrance on the stage refers to his *"appalling temper."* The character described is that of a man who has obtained mastery over his own passions and thus, according to Socrates, fitted himself for the task of governing others:

> *The lifelong struggle of a benevolent temperament and a high conscience against impulses of inhuman ridicule and fierce impatience has set up a chronic strain . . . He is a most implacable, determined, tenacious, intolerant person who by mere force of character presents himself as— and indeed actually is—considerate, gentle, explanatory, even mild and apologetic, capable possibly of murder, but not of cruelty or coarseness.*

Cusins has his proper place in Lady Britomart Undershaft's library. Its decorum, reflecting her own majestic rejection of all license, is an essential adjunct to its perfect security; she is herself prepared to recognise the dependence of the standards of a gentleman upon the tradition of classical education.

The significance of Cusins' crucial decision to accept a directorship in the Undershaft firm, in order to "make war on war," can be explored in terms of the rest of the passage from *The Birth of Tragedy,* which grows now even more closely analogous to the play than in its earlier sentences:

> This opposition became more precarious and even impossible, when from out of the deepest root of the Hellenic nature, similar impulses finally broke forth and made way for themselves: the Delphic god, by a seasonably effected reconciliation, was now contented with taking the destructive arms from the hands of his powerful antagonist. The reconciliation marks the most important moment in the history of the Greek cult: wherever we turn our eyes we may observe the revolutions resulting from

this event. It was the reconciliation of two antagonists, with the sharp
demarcation of the boundary-lines to be thenceforth observed by each
. . . in reality, the chasm was not bridged over. But if we observe how,
under the pressure of this conclusion of peace, the Dionysian power
manifested itself, we shall now recognise, in the Dionysian orgies of the
Greeks, as compared with the Babylonian Sacæa and their retrogression
of man to the tiger and the ape, the significance of festivals of world-re-
demption and days of transfiguration. Not till then does nature attain
her artistic jubilee; not till then does the rupture of the *principium
Individuationis* become an artistic phenomenon. (*op. cit.*, pp. 30–31)

The crisis with which the play is specifically concerned has been
precipitated by the action of Barbara Undershaft, granddaughter of
the Earl of Stevenage, daughter of a millionaire capitalist, leaving
the Established Church of the established social order to join the
Salvation Army. The inheritance of power, itself the destructive
weapon, is kept in the family through the resolution and audacity
of her *fiancé*, who makes his pact with "Dionysos Undershaft," though
asserting still: "I repudiate your sentiments. I abhor your nature. I
defy you in every possible way." The glorious "transfiguration" which
ensues has its appropriate setting in the Garden City of Perivale St.
Andrews, blueprint for the millennium of social welfare, and its individual enactment in Barbara's change of mood: "She has gone
right up into the skies," says Cusins.

Proleptically, the new redemptive rites are represented in the play
before Cusins' decisive gesture is made. He himself is ritually prepared
for the crisis by an evening spent with Undershaft (shown in the film
version, alluded to in the stage play): "He only provided the wine. I
think it was Dionysos who made me drunk"; by implication, the
drunkenness was spiritual and inspirational, not crudely orgiastic.
And the values the dramatist associates with the Salvation Army are
multiple, the morality of the soup kitchen, which Nietzsche-Under-
shaft rejects, being only tangential to it. The spirit of the Salvation
Army, as it has attracted Barbara Undershaft, is itself dionysiac and
revolutionary; but it is an enlightened and purified version of older,
cruder enthusiasms, which the Hellenistic mind is already able to ap-
prove and associate with from the start of the play; for Cusins, too,
though in pursuit of Barbara, has joined the Salvation Army. In his
apologia to Undershaft, he declares:

I am a sincere Salvationist. You do not understand the Salvation Army.
It is the army of joy, of love, of courage: it has banished the fear and
remorse and despair of the old hell-ridden evangelical sects: It marches
to fight the devil with trumpet and drum, with music and dancing, with
banner and palm, as becomes a rally from heaven by its happy garrison.
It picks the waster out of the public house and makes a man of him:
it finds a worm wriggling in a back kitchen, and lo! a woman! . . . It

takes the poor professor of Greek, the most artificial and self-sup-
pressed of human creatures, from his meal of roots, and lets loose the
rhapsodist in him . . .

In fact the reconciliation of Dionysos and Apollo enacted dramatically
in Act III is, in non-dramatic form, imaged from the first, already
achieved. Music, itself, is the sublimation of dionysiac energy. (The
full title of Nietzsche's famous essay is, of course: *The Birth of Tragedy
from the Spirit of Music.*)

Shaw actually stages the beginning of one triumphal procession and
accompanies it with a shadow-play of the supersession of one religion
by another. The form in which the climax, in Act II, is presented may
be related to another extract from *The Birth of Tragedy*:

> Schopenhauer has described to us the stupendous *awe* which seizes upon
> man, when of a sudden he is at a loss to account for the cognitive forms
> of a phenomenon, in that the principle of reason in some one of its
> manifestations, seems to admit of an exception. Add to this awe the bliss-
> ful ecstasy which rises from the innermost depths of man, ay, of nature,
> at this same collapse of the *principium individuationis,* and we shall gain
> an insight into the being of the *Dionysian,* which is brought within
> closest ken perhaps by the analogy of *drunkenness.* It is either under
> the influence of the narcotic draught, of which the hymns of all primitive
> men and peoples tell us, or by the powerful approach of spring penetrat-
> ing all nature with joy, that those Dionysian emotions awake, in the
> augmentation of which the subjective vanishes to complete self-forget-
> fulness. So also in the German Middle Ages singing and dancing crowds,
> ever increasing in number, were borne from place to place under this
> same Dionysian power. In these St. John's and St. Vitus's dancers we
> again perceive the Bacchic choruses of the Greeks, with their previous
> history in Asia Minor, as far back as Babylon and the orgiastic Sacaea.
> There are some, who, from lack of experience or obtuseness, will turn
> away from such phenomena as "folk-diseases" with a smile of contempt
> or pity prompted by the consciousness of their own health: of course, the
> poor wretches do not divine what a cadaverous-looking and ghastly
> aspect this very "health" of theirs presents when the glowing life of the
> Dionysian revellers rushes past them. (*op. cit.,* pp. 25–26)

With his presentation of the Salvation Army as a recrudescence of
Dionysiac fervour, Shaw extended Nietzsche's mediaeval analogues
to the bacchic chorus into modern times. The image suggested in the
last lines of Nietzsche's paragraph may have provided the hint for
the episode in which Barbara, who has just witnessed the triumph of
Undershaft at which her faith, as it seems, has crumbled, remains a
still figure amid the animated scene as the Salvation Army band,
caught up in the exultation with Undershaft, marches off with music
to the great meeting:

Cusins (returning impetuously from the shelter with a flag and a trombone, and coming between Mrs. Baines and Undershaft). You shall carry the flag down the first street, Mrs. Baines *(he gives her the flag).* Mr. Undershaft is a gifted trombonist: he shall intone an Olympian diapason to the West Ham Salvation March. *(Aside to Undershaft, as he forces the trombone on him.)* Blow, Machiavelli, blow. . . . It is a wedding chorus from one of Donizetti's operas; but we have converted it. . . . "For thee immense rejoicing—immenso giubilo—immenso giubilo." *(With drum obbligato)* Rum tum ti-tum-tum, tum tum ti ta—

Barbara. Dolly: you are breaking my heart.

Cusins. What is a broken heart more or less here? Dionysos Undershaft has descended. I am possessed. . . . Off we go. Play up, there. I m - m e n s o   g i u b i l o. *(He gives the time with his drum; and the band strikes up the march, which rapidly becomes more distant as the procession moves briskly away.)*

Mrs. Baines. I must go, dear. Youre overworked: you will be all right tomorrow. We'll never lose you. Now Jenny: step out with the old flag. Blood and Fire! *(She marches out through the gate with her flag.)*

Jenny. Glory Hallelujah! *(flourishing her tambourine and marching).*

Undershaft (to Cusins, as he marches out past him easing the slide of his trombone). "My ducats and my daughter!"

Cusins (following him out). Money and gunpowder!

Barbara. Drunkenness and Murder! My God: why hast thou forsaken me? *She sinks on the form with her face buried in her hands. The march passes away into silence.*

The exclamatory dialogue contributes to the excitement; the syntax of logical speech has little place here. The crescendo of sound is intensified by the gathering in of themes, the drawing together of the various symbolic perspectives in which Shaw presents his fable during the course of the play. But the sense of emotional and mental violence communicated at this point comes chiefly from the harshly ironic intersection of moods of exhilaration and agony. Horror at the contemplation of destructive power is transformed through identification with that power; pity is rejected for recognition of agony as a further inverted celebration of violent energy.[7] Shaw had perhaps remembered that comedy and tragedy alike have been traced back to the satyr chorus of the Dionysiac festival. There is no doubt that audiences are infected by the exhilaration. The conventional reaction to the sentimental appeal of a deserted heroine is pressed into service to give a keener edge to Cusins' brutal denial of sympathy and em-

---

[7] I find the effect comparable to that produced by Shelley's "Ode to the West Wind," except that the poem conveys a felt agony, while Shaw's words represent an agony in which the dramatist does not seem to participate.

phatic reassertion of unmixed joy.[8] We should like to recoil from him, but cannot. The experience is schizophrenic: a brilliantly conceived vehicle for the sense of loss of self-possession in a transport of irrational feeling. Shaw is demonstrating something very like a physical law: the superior power of volume of sound, weight of numbers releasing energy under the pressure of an intensifying rhythm. And the march remains a wedding march as the gentle-mannered Cusins confronts the chagrin of a subdued Barbara with a bridegroom's self-regarding exultation.

Yet the impression of the single figure in its stillness persists: there is strength of another kind in this maintained integrity and isolation. It is the apollonian will in Barbara that holds out now. And with the shock of recognising in her final cry, "My God: why hast thou forsaken me?" the words of the Christian divine saviour, the audience is returned to thoughtfulness.

"There are mystical powers above and behind the three of us," declares Undershaft in the screen version. The shadows of Dionysos and Apollo are to be glimpsed shiftingly behind Undershaft himself, Cusins and Barbara, but Barbara alone is the Christ figure of the play:[9] its action represents her ministry, her betrayal and abandonment by her disciples, and her agony; leaving off the uniform of the Army is a kind of death; visiting the munitions factory of Undershaft and Lazarus, she harrows hell; the multiple symbolism of the play's final setting suggests, as Shaw chooses to bring the various implications dramatically to life: Golgotha, in the dummy corpses of mutilated soldiers; the exceeding high mountain of the temptation; the mount of the resurrection, with a view of the New Jerusalem itself, where Peter Shirley has been given the job of gatekeeper and timekeeper.

Shaw, indeed, introduced a valid criticism of Nietzsche when he identified the Salvation Army not only with the worshippers of Dionysos, but also with the Church Militant of the risen Christ. His representation of Christianity as a variety of dionysiac religion corrects Nietzsche's exaggeration of its "objective" quality, which made possible his over-schematic view of the opposition between Christianity and Dionysos-Antichrist. The Preface to *Major Barbara* distinguishes between true Christianity and Crosstianity, the religion of negation, of sin and guilt, suffering and death, submission and deprivation. Within the play, a process of redemption is enacted through a bar-

[8] Nietzsche, of course, associates gloom with Dionysos, joy with the compact between dionysiac and apollonian powers.

[9] She is the daughter of Britomart, which being interpreted is "the sweet virgin," and, when the play opens, does not know her father. Shaw's study of Frazer shows here as in *Candida*.

gaining for souls and a vicarious sacrifice. It is a redemption of Christianity itself. Undershaft does not destroy the Salvation Army; he is ready partly to identify himself with it, more ready to identify it with himself, as, in order to win Barbara, he buys it with his cheque to Mrs. Baines, the Commissioner. Barbara's spiritual pilgrimage takes her through disillusion and despair to a rebirth of hope and a new vision. Her private emotional experience enforces the recognition that "the way of life lies through the factory of death," that destruction has its proper place in a healthy scheme of things, and even religion and morality must change in order to survive.[10] Her spiritual death and resurrection contain the promise of a new social order: the money for which she was betrayed bought the freedom of Bill Walker's soul. What this freedom implies is given rational definition in Cusins' declaration of his own new-found purpose:[11]

> I now want to give the common man weapons against the intellectual man. I love the common people. I want to arm them against the lawyers, the doctors, the priests, the literary men, the professors, the artists, and the politicians, who, once in authority, are more disastrous and tyrannical than all the fools, rascals and imposters.[12] I want a power simple enough for common men to use, yet strong enough to force the intellectual oligarchy to use its genius for the general good.

The purging of obsolete and unworthy elements in Barbara's Christian faith is accompanied by revision of its liturgy. This process begins in Act I, when the household, except for Stephen, is seduced from family prayers to the more original and vital form of service conducted by Barbara in the drawing room. It opens to the strains of *"Onward, Christian Soldiers, on the concertina, with tambourine accompaniment."* The emblematic sword, which Undershaft has referred to as the sign of his works, is already at least as appropriate as the cross in the insignia of Barbara's religion; and Shaw certainly expected his audience to supply the remembrance of Christ's words, "I came not to send peace but a sword." Cusins' excuse to Lady Britomart is unserious in manner and may easily be taken as simple camouflage; but rejecting, as it does, the terms of the General Confession, it at least calls into question the commonsense of perfectionism and the morality of self-abasement and excessive emphasis on guilt:

[10] Probably the best known lines in the play are Undershaft's: ". . . you have made for yourself something that you call a morality or a religion or what not. It doesnt fit the facts. Well, scrap it. Scrap it and get one that does fit."
[11] There may be some parallels of thought and idea with Yeats's *Calvary*, also indebted to Nietzsche.
[12] The Platonic view seems to have been adopted in order to be abandoned.

162

. . . you would have to say before all the servants that we have done things we ought not to have done, and left undone things we ought to have done, and that there is no health in us. I cannot bear to hear you doing yourself such an injustice, and Barbara such an injustice. As for myself, I flatly deny it: I have done my best.

Undershaft later proposes a revision in the Church Catechism to admit that "Money and gunpowder" are the "two things necessary to Salvation." His account of the works of mercy follows from an identification of the deadly sins with the burdensome material necessities of "Food, clothing, firing, rent, taxes, respectability and children." Stephen, in Act I, supplies the address of the Undershaft business as "Christendom and Judea." This serves as a warning note of a half-hidden movement in the play from the Old Testament (and ancient Greek) morality of just exchange to the New Testament morality of forgiveness and love. In effect, these are reconciled, through the rejection of false and facile interpretations of the New Testament admonitions. Cusins' point of agreement with Undershaft, "forgiveness is a beggar's refuge. I am with you there: we must pay our debts," [13] is the necessary counterpoise to that repudiation of irrational guilt in Act I (quoted at the top of the page). Cunningly, Undershaft confounds his daughter in answering her charge: "Father do you love nobody?" by carrying the meaning of love to the extreme of "Love your enemies":

> *Undershaft.* I love my best friend.
> *Lady Britomart.* And who is that, pray?
> *Undershaft.* My bravest enemy. That is the man who keeps me up to the mark.[14]

Cusins' admiring response to this, "You know, the creature is really a sort of poet in his way," does more than acknowledge the Socratic unfolding of neglected truth in a paradox; it conveys a recognition of beauty in the healthy ambivalence of strong emotions, an admission very necessary in the lover of Barbara that aggression need not be ugly and mean. His repudiation of beggarly forgiveness prepares for her new version of the Lord's Prayer:

[13] Cf. Bill Walker: "Let wot Aw dan be dan an pide for; and let there be an end of it." This is one point where the professor can appropriately point out that the modern Cockney thinks and acts like an ancient Greek. But Bill's attempt to buy his way out of obligations to practice the virtues of mercy and forbearance is no denial of those virtues. (Cusins and Barbara do not cease to value them, and indeed they are implied in Shaw's blueprint for the millennium, as presented in the last Act of the play.) This is just a stage in the process of his rehabilitation.

[14] Cf. Blake's "Opposition is True Friendship." Shaw is certainly fulfilling Blake's promise: "Note—This Angel, who is now become a Devil, is my particular friend; we often read the Bible together in its infernal or diabolical sense, which the world shall have if they behave well." (*The Marriage of Heaven and Hell*)

I have got rid of the bribe of bread. I have got rid of the bribe of heaven. Let God's work be done for its own sake: the work he had to create us to do because it cannot be done except by living men and women. When I die, let him be in my debt, not I in his; and let me forgive him as becomes a woman of my rank.[15]

This passes into an arrogance unjustified by the impression the character makes on us and itself unattractive.[16] For the most part, Shaw manages to endear to us a heroine whose actual living counterpart might well repel us. He does so by suffusing the portrait with his own warm appreciation of the type and setting it off by contrast with a minor sketch of a more conventionally admirable woman.

Orthodox Christianity has a truer representative in Jenny Hill, the Salvation Army lass, than in Barbara Undershaft, and Jenny's Christian spirit is a sublimation of her womanly nature. Jenny is the natural victim of the bullying male; turning the other cheek in response to Bill Walker's assault, offering forgiveness instead of revenge and treating her suffering as matter for joy. She merits her place in the triumphal band, bearing her tambourine, for she has positive qualities that Shaw admires: genuine courage and cheerfulness and industry in the cause she has at heart; this is a credible instance of the "worm in the back kitchen" become a woman, a daughter of the Highest. But Jenny's morale (she is only 18) is fed by her admiration of Barbara, and there are weaknesses in her that lessen her appeal. Her conventional expressions of piety often strike a false note; her insistence on *love* is too facile; her pity is equally sentimental. Neatly, Shaw demonstrates something unpleasant in her excessive sympathy: Barbara's sense of the ridiculous, like Undershaft's antagonisms, conveys a truer respect for human dignity, for the independence and privacy of the soul:

> Bill (*with some mirthless humour*). Aw was sivin anather menn's knees at the tawm. E was kneelin on moy ed, e was. . . . E was pryin for me: pryin camfortable wiv me as a cawpet. Sow was Mog. Sao was the aol bloomin meetin. Mog she sez "Aw Lawd brike is stabborn sperrit; bat downt urt is dear art." Thet was wot she said. "Downt urt is dear art!" An er blowk—thirteen stun four!—kneelin wiv all is wight on me. Fanny, aint it?
>
> Jenny. Oh no. We're so sorry, Mr. Walker.
>
> Barbara (*enjoying it frankly*). Nonsense! of course it's funny . . .
>
> Jenny. I'm so sorry, Mr. Walker.

[15] Cf. *The Marriage of Heaven and Hell:* "God only acts and is in existing beings or men."

[16] Yet it is a repellant quality, and an aggressiveness, far from unfamiliar in the militant virgin saints of Christian tradition.

Bill (fiercely). Downt you gow being sorry for me: youve no call. . . . Aw downt want to be forgive be you, or be ennybody . . .

If Shaw was concerned to attack the morbid sentimentality of late Victorian Christianity, he was—he needed to be—ready likewise to attack the womanly ideal associated with it. The imbalance between Jenny's emotional and intellectual development has made her the dupe of society, unawake to realities, assisting the millionaire's daughter in collecting the pennies of the indigent in her tambourine, as the wealthy good-for-nothing Lomax takes them in his hat. There is more of analogy than contrast to be drawn between her and Barbara, who, with the same power of work and need to expend herself in a cause, has to be cured of a similar blindness to things as they are, saved from an equal frittering away of her quality in a cause unliberated from a capitalist economy. Certainly G. B. S. does not repudiate wholesale the Christianity that Barbara and Jenny share; it is its vulnerability and self-betrayal that he rejects.

The whole play is flagrantly concerned with money. The first scene, set in the luxurious and stately library of the house in Wilton Crescent and dominated by the opulent physical presence of Lady Britomart, laps us round in an atmosphere of womblike security. The unreality of material need and adversity, in this context, comes through all the more clearly for Lady Britomart's talk of money and economy. If it were anxious talk, the whole effect would be destroyed; but there is no anxiety in Lady Britomart's make-up: she is the abundant and never-failing earth-mother of the peak of the golden year. In explaining to Stephen their financial situation, she is merely eliciting the moral approval she thinks due to her; she knows the easy and comfortable solution to her problems—such as they are!—and will apply it quite unscrupulously and without false pride; for she is free of the personal uncertainty that needs to worry about pride. In the first few minutes of the dialogue, we learn of the money available: the Lomax millions (though Charles will not inherit for 10 years); the "poverty" of the Earl of Stevenage on "barely seven thousand a year" and her own personal income, enough to keep one family in its present luxury. The date is 1906, and the value of the pound is high; anyway, Shaw has thoughtfully provided a cost-of-living index within the play: thirty-eight shillings a week is the standard wage paid by that model employer, Andrew Undershaft; in the first scene itself, her mother's standard of "poverty" can be measured against the reference to Barbara discharging her maid and living on a pound a week—a gesture with more of eccentricity, or even meanness, about it than real asceticism, for she still lives in Wilton Crescent and, when we see her, is the perfect representative of physical well-being: plump with nourishment, rosy-cheeked and "jolly" with health, brisk with energy. The immediate prospect is, perhaps, a little more serious for Sarah Undershaft and Charles Lomax, "poor as church mice" on £800 a year, as they are less richly endowed by nature. But there is always the comforting thought of the unseen providence who has only to be supplicated: the absent father, "rolling in money," "fabulously wealthy." Not a hint of the uncertainties of great wealth creeps into the dialogue, no shadow of sudden losses and bankruptcies, only of the chances of picking up a fortune. In every generation since the reign of James I some foundling has succeeded to the vast Undershaft inheritance; "they were rich enough to buy land for their own children and leave them well provided for," apart from the main bequest. Through the centuries the wealth has been accumulating without a break, it seems. This play is certainly not haunted by the Malthusian nightmare.

Of course, its world is that of folk-lore and fairy tale, of Dick Whittington and Jack and the Beanstalk; a world of inexhaustible hoards of treasure, where straw can be spun into gold and geese lay golden eggs; a world ruled over by luck, and indulgent to its favourites: the young, the beautiful, the cheerful, the quick-witted and, not least, the hopeful stranger who carries off the prize from the legitimate heir. The conditions of the will made by Charles Lomax's father establish the genre: "if he increases his income by his own exertions, they may double the increase." [17] They reveal a principle of economic distribution that could be called naturalistic, though it is also familiar in Christian terms: "To him that hath shall be given"; the proposition is that the naturally endowed are fittest to control the resources of civilized society. *Major Barbara,* in its unfolding, extends the principle beyond economic bounds: power to the strong; authority to the commanding.

The fictional situations on which Shaw's plays turn are often absurd and fantastic. Their remoteness from credible actuality works curiously in alliance with the excessively rational element. The arbitrariness of the fable, as an excuse for the play, is flaunted: Shaw is not dramatizing a story with a moral, but creating a dramatic image of his conflicting emotions and ideas. The blatant casuistry with which Cusins matches the doubtful relevance of the test—claimants for the Undershaft inheritance must prove that they are foundlings —communicates the dramatist's sense of logic as a game, his mind's self-delight in its own free play, and a scorn for the plodding literalist. Casuistry is a common element in fairy tales. But the foundling-motif

[17] Cf. *The Millionairess.*

is not without serious significance.[18] In relation to Shaw's own psyche, the foundling figure (recurrent in his drama) is interestingly linked with the images of providential bounty and the blueprint for a paternalist society. The conversion of Barbara, on which the play turns, is essentially conversion to the acceptance of wealth. As part of Shaw's campaign against idealism, or more precisely "Impossibilism" as he liked to term it, *Major Barbara* sets itself against false pride in unrealizable commodities. Beyond the temptation to refuse tainted money lies the more pernicious temptation to keep out of the market-place altogether. The position from which Cusins has begun to emerge in pursuit of Barbara, when the play begins, represents the negation from which he and Barbara have to be saved: the retirement of the intellectual, poet, or saint, possible only as a form of privilege (Oxford—surely it is Oxford?—being in 1906 no more an exposed position in society, no less comfortable, than Wilton Crescent, as Lady Britomart's acceptance of Cusins recognizes; scholars are gentlemen, and "nobody can say a word against Greek"). Shaw uses the character's intellectual clarity to make explicit, near the end of the play, the realist's view of selling the soul in compromise with the world:

> It is not the sale of my soul that troubles me: I have sold it too often to care about that. I have sold it for a professorship. I have sold it for an income. I have sold it to escape being imprisoned for refusing to pay taxes for hangmen's ropes and unjust wars and things that I abhor . . .

Before we reach this point, our acceptance of the statement as a truism has been prepared by Shaw's confrontation of the Faustian theme of the bargain with its connotations in the central Christian myth.

Undershaft as Mephistopheles, *doppelgänger* to Cusins' Faust, is presented as a sham villain in a sham conflict. He is more like Cusins than at first appears probable, the stage "heavy," but intellectualized, no more dionysian in temperament and character than Cusins, the self-confessed apollonian. The two together provide the play with twin foci of ironic consciousness, mutually comprehending; Undershaft merely reveals to Cusins what he already knows, in order to elicit admission of the knowledge: intellectually they are from the start equally free of illusions. They watch each other's manoeuvring for the winning—or betrayal—of Barbara (who is the Gretchen-Mar-

---

[18] It may be noted here that Lady Britomart and the foundling had had recent theatrical precursors in Wilde's Lady Bracknell and the child mislaid in a handbag. T. S. Eliot, remembering *The Importance of Being Earnest* in *The Confidential Clerk*, recognized that it was a farce on classical themes.

guerite of this aspect of the plot); they may talk of rivalry, but the total view they present is more like complicity.

It is in Act II, where Undershaft and Cusins observe the working out of the sub-plot, or inset play, involving Barbara and Bill Walker, that Shaw concentrates awareness of the Christian analogues: the price received by Judas for the betrayal of Christ and the sanctified bargain of the Redemption, the sacrifice which ransoms human souls. The act begins with the frauds, the minor characters of Rummy Mitchens and Snobby Price ("Snobby's a carpenter," says Rummy, so preparing for our recognition of the fullness of Bill Walker's pun: "Wot prawce selvytion nah? Snobby Prawce! Ha! Ha!").[19] Both are unscrupulous in their readiness to benefit from the providence of the Salvation Army. (Rummy and Lady Britomart, it seems, are sisters under their skins.) They epitomize a natural way of regarding wealth, opposed to Peter Shirley's and Bill Walker's legalistic way. Peter talks conscientiously in terms of paying for what he gets and being himself paid a just price for what he gives. Bill, attempting legalistically to buy the natural freedom of his soul, throws his sovereign on the drum,[20] where it is followed by Snobby Price's cap; Snobby, the instinctive, unregenerate socialist, is a parasite on legality, as well as the self-justified petty thief preying on such master-thieves as Undershaft and Bodger. Barbara, alluding to Bill's "twenty pieces of silver" and suggesting that her father need contribute no more than another ten "to buy anybody who's for sale," gives the gesture its ironic ambiguity: in the miniature play, the ostensible object of the bargain is Bill's soul and Barbara is both tempter and cheapjack working up the bidding—"Don't lets get you cheap," as she works up the collection at Army meetings; the greater price paid for Barbara herself, in the cheque handed over to Mrs. Baines by Undershaft, cancels out Bill's payment and is the token of his release from his bond;[21] the second payment is not only a magnified reflection of the first, but its sacramental transfiguration. To be for sale is the condition common to the sinner and the saint.

The folk law, to which the Undershaft tradition adheres, bears a

---

[19] His full name is Bronterre O'Brien Price, commemorating the Dublin Chartist, editor of *The Poor Man's Guardian*. (Incidentally, Bronterre > Brunty > Brontë + Romala > Rummy + Shirley suggests that Shaw's mind was running on women novelists and women of genius in general.)

[20] What are the traditional associations of this gesture? Recruiting, I think, as money is passed over a drum, though for what army is problematical here. Undershaft's army is perhaps itself the Church Militant. The fairground auction? Betting? The Salvation Army did in fact (does?) collect money on the drum. Was this one of the customs they took over from secular militarism?

[21] Another recent dramatic model comes to mind here: Yeats's Countess Cathleen pledging her soul in exchange for the lesser souls already bought by the devils.

genuine relation to the mythology at the centre of the play and to the ritual of the Dionysiac festivals in which Attic drama is believed to have originated, ritual celebrations of the rebirth of God in a divine foundling. In the present Shavian context, official Christianity is certainly reborn as natural religion after the symbolic "death" of Barbara. But there is also present the suggestion of a foundling Apollo inheriting from Dionysos.[22] The transmutation of this into the fairy tale of the boy from Australia who takes up the challenge and proves himself worthy of the kingdom and the hand of the princess, that traditionally go together, does much to save *Major Barbara* from pretentiousness. It also limits its powers to disturb. For despite its allusions to war, destruction and suffering, because it *is* a sophisticated fairy tale, *Major Barbara* is a rather comfortable play. Its concern with economics and the class structure of society, while bringing the fairy tale up-to-date, is itself subdued to fairy tale conventions. The genuineness of Shaw as a popular dramatist rests, it might be claimed, on the fact that he believed in fairy tales and transferred the element of wish-fulfilment they embody into a seemingly disillusioned drama. The play's movement from drawingroom comedy of family life into social *pièce-à-thèse* corresponds to Barbara's plea for "larger loves and diviner dreams than the fireside ones"; but the public world for which domesticity is repudiated, although more abstract, an area for the sublimation of private emotions, has itself a domestic[23] security assured by money.

Major Barbara is no exception to the tendency of Shaw's plays to reflect the pantomime form of fairytale material. There is a touch of that sham villain, the demon king, about Undershaft; and in the grouping of Lady Britomart and Barbara there is an intriguing resemblance to the association of the pantomime Dame with the Principal Boy.[24] In the course of the play, a number of references are made to Barbara's self-evident likeness to her mother. The most broadly comic is assigned to Lady Britomart herself in the opening scene:

[22] Cf. Note 1 to Gilbert Murray's "Excursus on the Ritual Forms Preserved in Greek Tragedy," in Jane Harrison's *Themis* (Meridian Books), p. 341: "It is worth remarking that the Year-Daimon has equally left his mark on the New Comedy. The somewhat tiresome foundling of unknown parentage who grows up, is recognized, and inherits, in almost every play of Menander that is known to us, is clearly descended from the foundling of Euripidean tragedy who turns out to be the son of a god and inherits a kingdom." Jane Harrison herself, *op. cit.* p. 443, suggests that Apollo and Dionysos are Kouroi and Year Gods "caught and in part crystallized at different stages of development."

[23] Cf. quotation below, p. 86.

[24] Cf. *Saint Joan*, in which the transvestite Principal Boy speaks pantomime-rustic, and is associated with the Ogres, Baudricourt and old Gruff-and-Grum Tremouille, Bluebeard, a comic Prince and such pantomime incidents as the marvel of the laying hens.

Ever since they made her a major in the Salvation Army she has developed a propensity to have her own way and order people about which
quite cows me sometimes. It's not ladylike: I'm sure I don't know where
she picked it up.

The whole of this scene is an emphatic demonstration of Lady Britomart's matriarchal domination of her son, Stephen. She accuses him
of fiddling first with his *"tie,"* then with his *"chain,"* and the objects
are certainly emblematic of his relations with her. The trick is later
repeated in her scene alone with Undershaft:

> *Lady Britomart.* Andrew: you can talk my head off; but you cant change
> wrong into right. And your tie is all on one side. Put it straight.
> *Undershaft (disconcerted).* It wont stay unless it's pinned (*he fumbles at
> it with childish grimaces*).

Here Andrew takes on the aspect of Jove in a nineteenth-century
classical burlesque, bullied by his consort. The parental reconciliation
which seems implied in the last Act denotes more than the acceptance
by society of an unpalatable truth, the reconciliation between power
and the "incarnation of morality." When Undershaft has won his
daughter, his wife sweeps in to appropriate the empire he has built
up.[25] The last glimpse we are given of Barbara represents her clutch-
ing "like a baby at her mother's skirt."

In retrospect, the action of the play, initiated by Lady Britomart,
can be seen as the working-out of her purpose: to absorb and assimi-
late the potentially hostile forces, adding them to her own strength.
Nations are revitalized in this way; and who else but Britannia have
we here? But the persistent victory of the mother over her children,
her power always to *contain* them, is more ambiguous in its value.
Barbara claims to take a less narrowly domestic and material view
than her mother—

> I felt like her when I saw this place—felt that I must have it—that
> never, never, never could I let it go; only she thought it was the houses
> and the kitchen ranges and the linen and the china, when it was really
> all the human souls to be saved . . .

but she is equally possessive, and her similar tendency to treat men
as children implies that the pattern will continue in the next generation. She addresses her *fiancé* invariably by the pet name of "Dolly"
(Lady Britomart, with the formality of her period, calls him reprov-
ingly: "Adolphus"); even when he has seemingly passed the test of
manhood by accepting Undershaft's challenge, he remains to Barbara:
"Silly baby Dolly," and she can cry exultantly: "I have my dear little

---

[25] Cf. the ostentatious ease and sangfroid with which the attractive, but indolent,
Sarah seats herself on the cannon.

Dolly boy still; and he has found me my place and my work." The
child keeps the doll, the mother keeps the child, the Stevenages maintain their ascendancy through the instrumentality of the strangers they
annex. In plays of the ironic mode, characters who never emerge from
behind the scenes are powerfully enigmatic and extend a sense of
ironic reaches beyond the limits of the dramatic frame. The Earl of
Stevenage, Lady Britomart claims, suggested the inviting of Andrew
to Wilton Crescent. Whether we take this eponymous ancestor of the
conventionally philistine Stephen to be a smokescreen or an actual
presence in the background, the sense of ulterior motivation remains
and the sense of a consciousness, like the author's, foreseeing and em-
bracing the whole dramatic development. Bill Walker warns Cusins
of the fate before him, as he relates his own experience of Barbara
to what may be in store for her "bloke":

> Gawd elp im! Gaw-aw-aw-awd elp im! . . . Awve aony ed to stend it
> for a mawnin: e'll ev to stend it for a lawftawm.

Martin Meisel has classified Barbara's wooing of Bill Walker's soul
as an example of the reversed love-chase (in which the woman is the
pursuer). Certainly it offers a reflection of, or insight into, Cusins'
role in the relationship which prefigures the greater metaphysical
marriage of Heaven and Hell. It is in relation to Bill that we chiefly
see demonstrated her capacity for chivvying and bullying, and Shaw
leaves us in no doubt of the hidden pressures on her side: her self-
confidence is the manner of her class, the product of money, of social
prestige and the habit of authority, the certainty of police protection
and support. What subdues Bill, before ever Barbara appears to him,
is the information that she is an Earl's granddaughter; when her
millionaire father turns up, he involuntarily touches his cap; the
brute force and skill of Todger Fairmile, already won over to Barbara's faith, are her final weapons. Bill's vulnerability to the woman's
ethic of respect for weakness, shame and guilt, which his blow to
Jenny Hill's face was an attempt to repudiate, is recognizably cari-
catured in the boastful "Snobby" Price, whose official confession, "how
I blasphemed and gambled and wopped my poor old mother," is bal-
anced by his private admission to Rummy, "She used to beat me,"
and who runs out the back way when his mother arrives at the gate.
For a moment near the end of Act II Bill is able to approach the
desolate Barbara with the magnanimity and good humour of an equal,
restored to freedom. But the image of Bill projected in Act III, is of
a man civilized into the middle class society of Perivale St. Andrews,
drawn, as Cusins is drawn, into the service of an established system.
    The method of constructing a play on analogies and reflections
leads to a recognition of the total unity in the author's mind, which

has been separated out and projected in the variety of characters. Shaw's total theme, in all its intricacy, may be suggested in symbols and symbolical gestures: the drum which beats with the pulse of life itself; the casting of the money on the drum, with no attempt to un- ravel rationally and conclusively the relation between wealth and power, possession and destruction. The extent to which the characters move in interrelation, now opposed to each other, now masking each other, seeming momentarily about to coalesce,[26] indicates the fineness of perception, the capacity for modifying and qualifying, doubting as well as forcefully asserting, that Shaw brought to his thought about social issues. His characters are ravished with admiration of Perivale St. Andrews, but mistrust is voiced, too. Barbara is aware that an effi- cient industrial society, however prosperous, is not the fulfilment of her vocation but its opportunity: Bill Walker as one of the "fullfed, quarrelsome, snobbish, uppish creatures" is not yet saved. The many churches in the city are not only confirmation of the comparative mythology built into the play, they represent rival visions and issues undecided. There is nothing static about this society: snobbery and the sense of hierarchy thrive, but they are confronted by the prin- ciples of the William Morris Labor Church. Significantly, the last line of the dialogue is an alert:

> *Undershaft (to Cusins).* Six o'clock tomorrow morning, Euripides.

Marrying Heaven and Hell requires eternal vigilance.

[26] Martin Meisel notes an approximation to an incest theme in Undershaft's wooing of his daughter; certainly it is representative of the intimacy in which the natures and destinies of all the characters seem connected.

The Wit and Satire of George Bernard Shaw

by Fred Mayne

Structure

In his reaction from the "well-made" play, Shaw thought, or pretended to think, that his plays had no construction. Nevertheless, plays which involve the proving of a thesis and not the unfolding of a plot often assume a pattern similar to that of the Socratic Method, which also has the proof of a view contrary to received opinion as its aim. There is a first stage, in which there is a general acceptance by most of the characters of the everyday or unparadoxical standpoint. This may or may not be accompanied by the celebrated Socratic Irony, in which the representative of the paradoxical view simulates ignorance and a touching desire to learn. The second and longest stage, the Definition, consists of a gradual and empirical revelation of the worthlessness of the accepted and the soundness of the paradoxical view. The third stage, the Maieutic, sets forth the implications of the new standpoint. The three stages in Shaw's plays are perhaps more mutually interpenetrative than the exposition, complication and dénouement of the drama of action or the three corresponding stages in the Socratic Dialogue. A Shavian play cannot be reduced to a formula.[1] Nevertheless, for a great number of the plays such a frame of reference is apparent. *Major Barbara,* with its highly paradoxical theme that money is the root of all virtue and that poverty is "the worst of all crimes," [2] provides a useful testing ground.

The first, or Irony stage, consists of a statement of the orthodox point of view as represented by Lady Britomart, whose objection to her husband is that he does not keep up the appearances required by

---

From The Wit and Satire of George Bernard Shaw *by Fred Mayne (New York: St. Martin's Press, 1967), pp. 42–44, 10–15, 89–90, 91–93, 96–98, 100–101, 124, 125–126. Reprinted by permission of St. Martin's Press, Inc., and Edward Arnold, Ltd.*

[1] See, for example, the varied interpretations of *Candida* as set out in Arthur H. Nethercot, *Men and Supermen,* Cambridge (Massachusetts), 1954, pp. 7–17.

[2] *Major Barbara,* Act III, p. 498.

conventional morality; by her son Stephen, a naïve moral absolutist whose objection to his father is that he is a social pariah for making millions out of selling cannons; by Barbara who represents the Christian standpoint that poverty is no bar to the purity of heart necessary to salvation; and by Cusins, a Greek scholar, who represents the humanism of Oxford and West Ham.

Even in this Irony stage the beginnings of the Definition stage can be seen; Stephen is a pretentious prig and Lady Britomart a hypocrite, though amiable and almost self-acknowledged. Barbara and Cusins, however, are presented in a favourable light; for the conversion to the paradoxical point of view, to be effective, must be an intellectual *tour de force* and not merely the overcoming of silly prejudices. For this reason, too, Shaw sweeps aside the usual plea that "the more destructive war becomes, the sooner it will be abolished." [3] Such a spuriously moral defence would make the fundamental paradox less forceful.

Undershaft, the arms manufacturer, is the protagonist of the paradoxical point of view, and the exponent of what Lady Britomart calls a "religion of wrongness." [4] He has "an engaging simplicity of character," [5] is quite submissive to his wife, and is diffident and deferential in manner to everybody. "Never mind me, my dear. As you know, I am not a gentleman; and I was never educated." [6] He has the *ingénu* attitude of Socrates which we have already noticed in Lady Cicely in *Captain Brassbound's Conversion,* and, by the end of the first act he has on a purely personal plane won over the younger generation to such an extent that Lady Britomart even talks about fathers who come along and steal the children's affections from the mother.[7]

The second, or Definition stage, is divided into two parts. Act II, set in the yard of a Salvation Army shelter, ends in the debacle of the Christian position, with Barbara saying "My God: why hast thou forsaken me?" [8] and "Peter: I'm like you now. Cleaned out, and lost my job." [9] Act III, set partly in Lady Britomart's residence and partly in Undershaft's arms foundry, sees first the dialectical rout of Stephen and then a practical vindication of Undershaft's views in the form of the model community dependent on the manufacture of arms. It must be borne in mind that only a structural comparison with Socratic Method is being made. Detachment and an exhaustive elimination mark the Definition stage in Socrates, whereas Shaw, both by tem-

[3] *Ibid.,* Act I, p. 468.   [7] *Ibid.,* Act I, p. 470.
[4] *Ibid.,* Act I, p. 463.   [8] *Ibid.,* Act II, p. 485.
[5] *Ibid.,* Act I, p. 466.   [9] *Ibid.,* Act II, p. 486.
[6] *Ibid.,* Act I, p. 467.

perament and dramatic necessity, immediately whisks his audiences
off to grounds of his own choosing.

The Maieutic stage sees the conversion of Cusins and Barbara to
the paradoxical view, propounded anew by Cusins: "Then the way
of life lies through the factory of death?" [10] And so that once again
nothing may lessen the force of the paradox, the conversion comes
after Undershaft has told them of the good news from Manchuria
about a new aerial battleship which has wiped out a fort with three
hundred soldiers in it. "To be wealthy," says Undershaft, "is with me
a point of honor for which I am prepared to kill at the risk of my
own life. This preparedness, is, as he says, the final test of sincerity." [11]
The implication of the Definition stage in *Major Barbara* is that we
can only work to a higher end through reality, through institutions
as they are, through human beings who are as yet imperfectly developed, and that it is useless to build Utopias on absolutist sands.
For paradox, as a form of wit, is rational in conception and intention
and exposes the sham and immorality which often lie concealed behind received opinion and taboo morality.

Style

. . . The rapid flow of Shaw's prose is of course mainly achieved by
assiduous attention to rhythm. Now, not all humorous writing requires a rapid tempo. Deprecatory humour and humour which depends on a simulated ingenuousness and earnestness may require a
more halting rhythm, varied perhaps by little ridiculous rushes of
confidence. The humour, too, which is combined with pathos must
obviously suit the tempo to the mood. Polemical wit, however, must
be delivered at great speed in order to preserve an appearance of
confident objectivity and to promote that suspension of judgement so
important to its success. The voluble and vivacious patter of Sullivan's
music is the musical counterpart to, and the setting for, the satirical
frivolity of Gilbert. Shaw not only provides a musical counterpart to
his own wit, but also makes the most of the humour of the inevitable
which is inherent in regular rhythm. It is not surprising that serious
poetry with a too regular beat, so suitable for comic verse, easily slips
into bathos and lends itself so well to parody. . . .

"Do not suppose for a moment," said Shaw, "that I learnt my art
from English men of letters. True, they showed me how to handle
English words; but if I had known no more than that, my works would

[10] *Ibid.*, Act III, p. 503.
[11] *Major Barbara*, Prefaces, p. 120.

never have crossed the Channel. My masters were the masters of a universal language; they were, to go from summit to summit, Bach, Handel, Haydn, Mozart, Beethoven and Wagner." [12] It is significant that the final "summit" is Wagner, whom Shaw described as "the literary musician par excellence," [13] because his subject matter was so closely allied to his tone structures.

* * *

The use of rhetorical rhythm was particularly dangerous for one who aimed at intellectual rather than emotional conversion. Rhythm exerts a hypnotic spell, evoking responses almost at a biological level. Nevertheless, as with alliteration and assonance, it is used far more freely in the speeches of his witty and proselytizing realists who give the Shavian viewpoint than in the speech of the romantics; for self-expression naturally took the form of wit. Tanner's speeches are wittier and more rhythmical than Ramsden's or Octavius's, Don Juan's than the Statue's, Undershaft's than Stephen's, Magnus's than Boanerges's, and those of the realistic realist, Larry Doyle, than those of the romantic realist, Tom Broadbent. Characters representing the opposition seldom use the rhythmic rhetoric which is so often the vehicle for Shaw's satiric powers of persuasion:

> *Stephen (springing up again)*. I am sorry, sir, that you force me to forget the respect due to you as my father. I am an Englishman; and I will not hear the government of my country insulted. (*He thrusts his hands in his pockets, and walks angrily across to the window.*)
> *Undershaft (with a touch of brutality)*. The government of your country! *I* am the government of your country: I, and Lazarus. Do you suppose that you and half a dozen amateurs like you, sitting in a row in that foolish gabble shop, can govern Undershaft and Lazarus? No, my friend: you will do what pays us. You will make war when it suits us, and keep peace when it doesnt. You will find out that trade requires certain measures when we have decided on those measures. When I want anything to keep my dividends up, you will discover that my want is a national need. When other people want something to keep my dividends down, you will call out the police and military. And in return you shall have the support and applause of my newspapers, and the delight of imagining that you are a great statesman. Government of your country! Be off with you, my boy, and play with your caucuses and leading articles and historic parties and great leaders and burning questions and the rest of your toys. *I* am going back to my counting-house to pay the piper and call the tune.

[12] Quoted by Wilson: *Triple Thinkers,* p. 173.
[13] "The Perfect Wagnerite" (1898), *Major Critical Essays,* 1947, p. 266.

Stephen (actually smiling, and putting his hand on his father's shoulder with indulgent patronage). Really, my dear father, it is impossible to be angry with you. You dont know how absurd all this sounds to me. You are very properly proud of having been industrious enough to make money; and it is greatly to your credit that you have made so much of it. But it has kept you in circles where you are valued for your money and deferred to for it, instead of in the doubtless very old-fashioned and behind-the-times public school and university where I formed my habits of mind. It is natural for you to think that money governs England; but you must allow me to think I know better.

Major Barbara, Act III, pp. 490–1.

With its "proud of having been," its "made so much of it," its "instead of in," and its "deferred to for it," Stephen's diligent misinterpretation stands in strong contrast to Undershaft's resonant rhetoric.

Not only does the style of speech suit the speaker, but it also varies widely in the same speaker. This does not mean that the characters necessarily speak out of character, but that they change under the pressure of a new situation or, as is more likely in Shaw, under the pressure of a new idea or challenge. The diffident Undershaft of the first Act is not the proselytizing Undershaft of the second and third Acts. Cusins, the detached and witty bystander of the beginning of the play, finally becomes Cusins, the convert. With these changes comes a change in the rhythm of their speeches. How out of character would have been the following rhetorical outburst from an unconverted Cusins:

Cusins. You cannot have power for good without having power for evil too. Even mother's milk nourishes murderers as well as heroes. This power which only tears men's bodies to pieces has never been so horribly abused as the intellectual power, the imaginative power, the poetic, religious power that can enslave men's souls. As a teacher of Greek I gave the intellectual man weapons against the common man. I now want to give the common man weapons against the intellectual man. I love the common people. I want to arm them against the lawyers, the doctors, the priests, the literary men, the professors, the artists, and the politicians, who, once in authority, are more disastrous and tyrannical than all the fools, rascals, and impostors. I want a power simple enough for common men to use, yet strong enough to force the intellectual oligarchy to use its genius for the general good.

Ibid., Act III, p. 502.

The wit is still there but it is now a wit informed by a more constructive purpose. It is the same kind of wit as that of the later Undershaft.

The more emphatic rhythm of the proselytizing realists is, of course, the vehicle for more effective assertion, for a rhetoric which, if broken into its elements, has the superficial appearance of invective. But it is raised far above the level of invective and declamation to high satire by the loftiness of the theme, by the intensity of moral feeling, and, what concerns us more at the moment, by the extraordinary skill with which the units of invective are built up into a glittering and imposing configuration. The rhythm contributes to the appearance of effortlessness and is the cement which binds the structure together. The result is what we may call an oratorical style.

Many discussions on Shaw's style recognise that it was shaped on the public platform, but forget that the stage is a public platform and that, stylistically, the distinguishing feature of written polemic is its oratorical form.

> Shaw had no patience with discussions concerning the niceties and secret subtleties of literary style. He insisted that in writing the one and only thing to aim at was effectiveness of assertion. . . . Shaw's most conspicuous fault was over-emphasis. It belonged to his method and was deliberately cultivated, and it is hard not to believe that the habit of it, a habit which grew, was largely born of the platform.[14]

Frank Harris called it "harangue-writing"[15] and estimated that during his Socialist period Shaw gave a thousand harangues in twelve years.[16]

Now such criticism is hardly legitimate unless we expect, for instance, irony in advertisement copy or wit in an obituary notice. Shaw either wrote frank polemic or he wrote for the stage, and dramatic dialogue demands an immediate response from an audience. This response is conditioned by the volatility of the spoken word, and by participation as a member of a by no means homogeneous group. Of a secluded reader a much more active, and therefore, imaginative response should be sought by means of a more indirect and allusive style. A reading of Shaw may at times produce a feeling of being bludgeoned into acquiescence by a continuous and wearisome violence of assertion; but listening to him in the auditorium, this "biting over-emphasis"[17] is effective in gaining unremitting attention to the spoken word. A similar feeling of fatigue and consequent decline in attention or mindfulness may perhaps be brought on by reading through Shakespeare's flood of metaphor, particularly in the later plays; but Shake-

---

[14] S. K. Ratcliffe, "Shaw as a Young Socialist," *Shaw and Society,* ed. C. E. M. Joad, 1953, pp. 63–4.

[15] Harris, p. 98.

[16] *Ibid.*, p. 93.

[17] Edmund Wilson, "Bernard Shaw on the Training of a Statesman," *Classics and Commercials,* 1951, p. 240.

speare's metaphor is less a poetic parallel than a corporeal substitute, and from the stage it is a marvellous means of bodying forth a complex situation. Even if Shaw, like Shakespeare, had not been careful to give his audiences a rest from his rhetorical fireworks, the sheer brilliance of the display would be almost enough to ensure unflagging attention.

Irony

To say that wit nearly always deals in half-truths or that the sphere of wit lies between falsehood and truth is another way of saying that wit deals in understatement and overstatement, the plain statement being the non-witty expression of the truth. If the understatement and the overstatement become so extreme that they say the opposite of what is meant, then the field of irony and sarcasm, on a verbal plane at any rate, has been entered. Sarcasm might almost be described as exaggerated overstatement and irony as exaggerated understatement. Fowler's distinction between sarcasm, which works through inversion, and irony, which works through mystification,[18] obscures this fundamental identity of the two spheres of wit; but it does indicate that irony, like understatement, is usually a far more indirect and therefore artistic form of wit than overstatement or sarcasm. In sarcasm the inversion is obvious, but in irony it is decorous and disguised. The difference in relation between speaker and listener is fundamental.

Consequently, verbal irony is not suitable for the stage; for, as has already been remarked, the spoken word demands an immediate response from the audience. The small circle of initiates to which irony addresses itself will dwindle to the playwright and his secretary if the irony is so delicate that it takes more than a moment to recognise, for the audience has no more than a moment to spare. Furthermore, Shaw, as Potts says, is not addressing "a public of aesthetes, scholars, or literary critics. The lack of 'art' with which Ben Jonson reproached Shakespeare has been vindicated, and I have little doubt that Mr. Shaw's will be vindicated too, when time has placed him in perspective." [19] There was in Shaw, too, none of what Herbert Read calls that "mean and esoteric spirit that lacks common understanding and sympathy," which makes irony "more often the weapon of an exclusive egotism," and "explains why it is used but sparingly by writers of true eloquence." [20] For Shaw the stage was no cave of Delphi but a public rostrum.

[18] H. W. Fowler, *A Dictionary of Modern English Usage,* second edition, revised by Sir Ernest Gowers, 1965, p. 253.

[19] Potts, p. 41.

[20] Herbert Read, *English Prose Style,* 1928, p. 190.

Dramatic desiderata, polemical necessity, and personal predilection would, then, all lead us to expect little verbal irony in Shaw. What little we do find is usually either what is known as "heavy irony," which is practically indistinguishable from sarcasm, or is underscored so thickly that it cannot be missed:

> Undershaft *(hugely tickled)*. You dont say so! What! no capacity for business, no knowledge of law, no sympathy with art, no pretension to philosophy; only a simple knowledge of the secret that has puzzled all the philosophers, baffled all the lawyers, muddled all the men of business, and ruined most of the artists: the secret of right and wrong. Why, man, youre a genius, a master of masters, a god! At twentyfour, too!
>
> *Major Barbara,* Act III, p. 490.

The irony is so heavy that it does not even deceive Stephen, an uncommonly common denominator.

                            *   *   *

One of Shaw's failings was to point his verbal irony far beyond even the requirements of the stage.

> Undershaft *(with a reasonableness which Cusins alone perceives to be ironical)*. My dear Barbara: alcohol is a very necessary article. It heals the sick—
>
> Barbara. It does nothing of the sort.
>
> Undershaft. Well, it assists the doctor: that is perhaps a less questionable way of putting it. It makes life bearable to millions of people who could not endure their existence if they were quite sober. It enables Parliament to do things at eleven at night that no sane person would do at eleven in the morning. Is it Bodger's fault that this inestimable gift is deplorably abused by less than one per cent of the poor? *(He turns again to the table; signs the cheque; and crosses it.)*
>
> Mrs. Baines. Barbara: will there be less drinking or more if all those poor souls we are saving come tomorrow and find the doors of our shelters shut in their faces? Lord Saxmundham gives us the money to stop drinking—to take his own business from him.
>
> Cusins *(impishly)*. Pure self-sacrifice on Bodger's part, clearly! Bless dear Bodger! *(Barbara almost breaks down as Adolphus, too, fails her.)*
>
> Undershaft *(tearing out the cheque and pocketing the book as he rises and goes past Cusins to Mrs. Baines)*. I also, Mrs. Baines, may claim a little disinterestedness. Think of my business! think of the widows and orphans! the men and lads torn to pieces with shrapnel and poisoned with lyddite! *(Mrs. Baines shrinks; but he goes on remorselessly)* the oceans of blood, not one drop of which is shed in a really just cause! the ravaged crops! the peaceful peasants forced, women and men, to till their fields under the fire of opposing armies on pain of starvation! the

bad blood of the fierce little cowards at home who egg on others to fight for the gratification of their national vanity! All this makes money for me: I am never richer, never busier than when the papers are full of it. Well, it is your work to preach peace on earth and goodwill to men. (*Mrs. Baines's face lights up again.*) Every convert you make is a vote against war. (*Her lips move in prayer.*) Yet I give you this money to help you to hasten my own commercial ruin. (*He gives her the cheque.*)

Cusins (*mounting the form in an ecstasy of mischief*). The millennium will be inaugurated by the unselfishness of Undershaft and Bodger. Oh be joyful! (*He takes the drumsticks from his pockets and flourishes them.*)

Mrs. Baines (*taking the cheque*). The longer I live the more proof I see that there is an Infinite Goodness that turns everything to the work of salvation sooner or later. Who would have thought that any good could have come out of war and drink? And yet their profits are brought to-day to the feet of salvation to do its blessed work. (*She is affected to tears.*)

Jenny (*running to Mrs. Baines and throwing her arms around her*). Oh dear! how blessed, how glorious it all is!

Cusins (*in a convulsion of irony*). Let us seize this unspeakable moment. Let us march to the great meeting at once. Excuse me just an instant. (*He rushes into the shelter. Jenny takes her tambourine from the drum head.*)

Mrs. Baines. Mr. Undershaft: have you ever seen a thousand people fall on their knees with one impulse and pray? Come with us to the meeting. Barbara shall tell them that the Army is saved, and saved through you.

Major Barbara, Act II, pp. 484–5.

Barbara's "It does nothing of the sort"; Cusin's "Pure self-sacrifice on Bodger's part"; Undershaft's widows, orphans, and shattered soldiers; Cusins's "The millennium will be inaugurated by the unselfishness of Undershaft and Bodger," all add weight to the verbal irony, which would be sinking under its own ballast in any literary medium other than the drama.

But the passage contains much more than verbal irony. It is the very stuff out of which drama is made. Undershaft and Cusins, ironists both, look through the simple world of Mrs. Baines and Barbara into the complex reality below. This complexity is best revealed in drama because complexity is often revealed by means of conflict; and conflict depends on the juxtaposition of opposites, which in its turn gives rise to an ironic antithesis sustained long enough to ensure a response from the audience. Mrs. Baines and even Barbara are simple souls who live in the Fool's Paradise of their own immediate preoccupation.

Undershaft and Cusins know that there is no Paradise except that of
the Fool. The skulls of human beings struck down by Drink and War
appear, not on Undershaft's but on Mrs. Baines's shoulder, and supply
their own grinning commentary.

Undershaft's defence is an inverted attack, an attack on sentimental
evasion and Ibsenite "idealism," the inversion being achieved by ally-
ing Guns and Alcohol with Salvation, ideas which in the creed of the
romantic are antagonistic to each other. Such "defences" are one of
the commonest weapons of the ironist.

Character

But, as already indicated in dealing with rhetoric in Shaw, and with
the passage in which Undershaft and Mrs. Baines are involved, it is
mainly through the juxtaposition of characters that drama dispenses
its ironic contrasts and reveals that man's claim to be a creature guided
by reason is a ridiculous and unsubstantiated pretension. The classic
contrast is, of course, between the Eiron and the Alazon. "This is the
confrontation in the earliest Greek comedy of the Ironist and the Impostor, the Ironist in Shaw being always the soft-spoken vital man in
harmony with himself, the Impostor being the professional man who
has ideologies and habits instead of ideas and impulses." [21] Here
Bentley once again makes an application of Bergson's thesis that rigidity of mind is the chief target of comic criticism. The Eiron eschews
emotion, and in doing so achieves the intellectual detachment necessary for the exercise of wit. In the Alazon, however, emotional and
inflexible patterns conditioned by false social ideals take precedence
over the intellect. The Eiron is placid, polite and deprecatory; while
the Alazon is energetic, bombastic, and dogmatic. The Alazon is raised
by his opponent's humility to a higher perch where he may be more
easily attacked, and from which his fall is correspondingly greater.

But in drama, particularly in sociological drama, the same degree
of detachment as we find in a Socratic *ingénu* or in a propitiatory
Chaucer is not practicable. Self-speaking truth is no more possible than
a too highly polished verbal irony. Some character or characters must
speak the truth, and so it is only in the expository stage of the play,
before the conflict has been joined, that the Eiron can be his anaemic
self. As Worcester says in *The Art of Satire*, "Irony delights in the collision of opposites" but it also "offers a way of escaping from the conflict and rising above it." [22] Bentley's "soft-spoken" ironist is too great
a simplification and, as has already been seen, the Undershaft of the

[21] Bentley, *Shaw*, p. 171.
[22] Worcester, p. 141.

beginning of the play is not the Undershaft of a later period. It is the vital man who has the gift of the gab, who is the master of rhetoric. Only if the vitalist is not primarily engaged in converting to realism but is converting from romanticism does he assume a mask of ironic diffidence.[23] Says Freud of Falstaff: "Sir John's own humor really emanates from the superiority of an ego which neither his physical nor his moral defects can rob of its joviality and security."[24] And it is this inner assurance, often expressing itself in alazonic joviality and pugnacity, which animates the so-called ironists of Shaw. There is none of the "understating of the whole personality"[25] which Worcester notes in Socratic irony. The triumph of the ironist who is in part impostor is paralleled in the play, inevitable in its outcome and unexpected in its wit.

> Andrew Undershaft comes in. All rise. Lady Britomart meets him in the middle of the room behind the settee.
>
> Andrew is, on the surface, a stoutish, easy-going elderly man, with kindly patient manners, and an engaging simplicity of character. But he has a watchful, deliberate, waiting, listening face, and formidable reserves of power, both bodily and mental, in his capacious chest and long head. His gentleness is partly that of a strong man who has learnt by experience that his natural grip hurts ordinary people unless he handles them very carefully, and partly the mellowness of age and success. He is also a little shy in his present very delicate situation.
>
> *Major Barbara*, Act I, p. 466.

In spite, perhaps, of Shaw's intentions, Undershaft's "kindly patient manners" last no longer than it takes him to make the acquaintance of his family. He defends his profession as "a profiteer in mutilation and murder" with unironic energy and throws down the gauntlet to Barbara almost immediately.

> *Undershaft.* May I ask have you ever saved a maker of cannons?
> *Barbara.* No. Will you let me try?
> *Undershaft.* Well, I will make a bargain with you. If I go to see you tomorrow in your Salvation Shelter, will you come the day after to see me in my cannon works?
> *Barbara.* Take care. It may end in your giving up the cannons for the sake of the Salvation Army.
> *Undershaft.* Are you sure it will not end in your giving up the Salvation Army for the sake of the cannons?
>
> *Ibid.*, Act I, p. 469.

Scarcely Socratic in method or manner. Indeed Shaw seems to feel

[23] See p. 27.
[24] Freud, Footnote, p. 377.
[25] Worcester, p. 95.

the necessity for a more minor character, Cusins, to supply an ironic commentary on Undershaft.

*   *   *

Bentley's application of the classic comic contrast to Shaw is, then, more valid when the realist is engaged in the more negative task of converting not to realism but from romanticism.

When the circumstances with which the individual finds himself in conflict are not merely those of the immediate situation but of his whole way of life, there arises a profounder type of irony such as has already been noticed in the Salvation Army refuelling with Bodger's whisky. There is this form of irony, too, in *Widowers' Houses* when Trench, after his condemnation of Sartorius, finds that his own income is equally tainted. There is irony in *Captain Brassbound's Conversion* when the Captain finds that his own moral position is little better than that of the man whom he is pursuing with righteous vengeance. There is irony in *Androcles and the Lion* when Spintho finds he is more afraid of being eaten by lions than going to Hell, but in the end suffers both. But in each example it is not dramatic irony. The audience knows no more about the equivocal position of the victim than the victim himself. Shaw's audience does not consist of the ironist's circle of initiates watching the character acting in ignorance of his own condition: it is made up of romantics who must also suffer conversion. The irony consists in the audience, as well as the stage characters, being hoist with their own petards.

An even profounder level of irony arises from the contemplation of the individual in conflict, not merely with his own way of life, but with life itself. He is at odds with something over which he has no control, over which no control is apparently possible. He is at odds with the limitations imposed on him by his own mortality; he is at odds with an organic society with its own laws of development and decay, whose ends are as impossible to shape as those of the individual organism. Confronted with this spiritual *impasse,* the ironist admits defeat, withdraws to the sidelines and watches the efforts of others to conquer or compromise with amused and even flippant detachment. The philosopher, on the other hand, seeks to escape, less by shaping individual ends, than by gathering them up into a higher synthesis. The contradiction that is Shaw can only be understood if one sees in him both the flippant ironist and the philosopher, who would overcome both the shortcomings of our finite lives and our corrupt society through the higher synthesis of Creative Evolution, which was, by its very remoteness in time, a doctrine of immediate despair.

Wit as Evasion

Ironic acceptance springs from a realisation of the powerlessness of humanity to control its own destiny. It will, in seeking expression, be closely allied to tragedy; for tragedy is a revelation of the greatest joke of all, with all mankind reduced to a state of puppetry. Nothing burlesques so well as tragedy; for just as comedy is close to tears when it mingles with pathos, so is tragedy close to laughter if the pathos is excluded and stark inevitability alone remains. It is laughter in its most elemental form, laughter at the discomfiture of another, laughter which springs from grim satisfaction that nobody, not even the most exalted, is exempt from the cruel working of time and fate. For in tragedy, inevitability is almost completely divorced from the unexpected; and whenever the factor of time intrudes itself as a dominant, uncontrollable, but not unpredictable factor, the work of art will usually be tragic in tone. Not that tragedy is necessarily the product of despair. The classic, cathartic, conception of tragedy implies ultimate hope and harmony. But there is no hope and no harmony when there is no catharsis, or when catharsis is attempted by a sudden reversion from ultimate implications to the more comfortable reassurances of comedy and its preoccupation with a more malleable, or potentially more malleable, present.

* * *

In *Major Barbara*, there is an evasion of the ultimately tragic consequences of the destruction of Cusins's humanism and Barbara's Christian ethic by an emphasis on the present:

Cusins (*overjoyed*). Then you—you—you——Oh for my drum! (*He flourishes imaginary drumsticks.*)

Barbara (*angered by his levity*). Take care, Dolly, take care. Oh, if only I could get away from you and from father and from it all! if I could have the wings of a dove and fly away to heaven!

Cusins. And leave me!

Barbara. Yes, you, and all the other naughty mischievous children of men. But I cant. I was happy in the Salvation Army for a moment. I escaped from the world into a paradise of enthusiasm and prayer and soul saving; but the moment our money ran short, it all came back to Bodger: it was he who saved our people: he, and the Prince of Darkness, my papa. Undershaft and Bodger: their hands stretch everywhere: when we feed a starving fellow creature, it is with their bread, because there is no other bread; when we tend the sick, it is in the hospitals they endow; if we turn from the churches they build, we must kneel

on the stones of the streets they pave. As long as that lasts, there is
no getting away from them. Turning our backs on Bodger and Undershaft is turning our backs on life.

Major Barbara, Act III, p. 502.

But Shaw, in refusing to turn his back on life in the present, was
turning his back on life in the future. The tragedy of Barbara's broken
heart was not averted by any genuine reconciliation between her
aspirations and her immediate fate. Barbara may be angered by
Cusins's levity and his flourishing of drumsticks, but it was an ironically mischievous assault on the drums that marked the beginning of
his conversion to Undershaftism:

> *Cusins.* It is a wedding chorus from one of Donizetti's operas; but we
> have converted it. We convert everything to good here, including
> Bodger. You remember the chorus. "For thee immense rejoicing—im-
> menso giubilo—immenso giubilo." (*With drum obbligato.*) Rum tum ti
> tum tum, tum tum ti ta——
> *Barbara.* Dolly: you are breaking my heart.
> *Cusins.* What is a broken heart more or less here? Dionysos Undershaft
> has descended. I am possessed.

Ibid., Act II, p. 485.

Comedy is used as a means of avoiding the fundamental conflict between the present and the eternal.

PART TWO

View Points

Eric Bentley

Generalizing from *Three Plays for Puritans,* some critics have assumed that *all* Shaw's plays show a vital hero surrounded by the victims of artificial system. Yet we have seen that this pattern is subtly inverted in *Man and Superman* and *Pygmalion* where—such is Shaw's version of the female and male principles—the heroine is the vital one and the hero only a vitalist. It is inverted also in *John Bull* where the central character is Broadbent who is a devout idealist and by that token the archetype of Shavian villainy. In *Major Barbara,* the central trio—Undershaft, Barbara, Cusins—differs as much from Broadbent, Keegan, and Doyle as from Ramsden, Ann, and Tanner. This time the successful man is a modern Caesar, at home with himself, imaginative in the Shavian sense, very much the vital hero. The idealistic heroine, though at the outset far gone in illusions, is jolted back to reality at the famous emotional climax of the play. The young professor of Greek who is to be Undershaft's successor will unite—we are asked to hope—realism and idealism, practicality and wisdom, in an almost superhuman union.

Such at any rate seems to be the intention of the play. It is not quite realized. Barbara's final conversion has much less force than her previous disillusionment. Undershaft remains far more impressive than Cusins. Seemingly Shaw started out to demonstrate that poverty is a crime and therefore that there is more good sense in the career of an Undershaft than in that of a Snobby Price. His play was to have been called *Andrew Undershaft's Profession,* presumably in ironic parallelism with *Mrs. Warren's Profession,* which showed exactly the opposite side of the truth. Probably the idea of making Cusins the synthesis of Barbara's idealism and her father's realism came to Shaw later, perhaps *too* late. His devil's advocacy remains all too effective. Like so many other writers, he makes his monster so impressive that no good man can match him. He so brilliantly proves that "money is the most important thing in the world" that he can-

From Bernard Shaw, *rev. ed., by Eric Bentley (New York: New Directions, 1957), pp. 166–68. Copyright 1947,* © *1957 by New Directions Publishing Corporation. Reprinted by permission of New Directions Publishing Corporation and Methuen & Co. Ltd. A third edition was published in 1967.*

not quite enforce the fundamental Shavian principle that selling your-self is the ultimate horror, that "money was not born in the light." Superficial observers have said that, though Shaw's early businessmen —Crofts, Burgess, Lickcheese—are rogues, his later ones—Undershaft, Tarleton—betray Shaw's growing conservatism. For Shaw, however, Undershaft and Tarleton are realities which he was trying to under-stand and do justice to. The businessman in a much later play— *Heartbreak House*—is also a rogue; in that play and in many to fol-low the original Shavian position is reaffirmed.

Not that *Major Barbara* was for Shaw a pure eccentricity. Its heroine for example is evidence of a new approach. In his earlier period Shaw had surprised his audience with two kinds of women: capable, unromantic women like Vivie, Candida, Lady Cicely, and acquisitive, passionate women like Mrs. Warren and Blanche Sar-torius. After the latter type has culminated in Ann Whitefield, it apparently ceases to be important for Shaw, reappearing only in such termagants as Hypatia and the Millionairess; the "mother woman" dies out. Even the self-possessed capable type is less frequent. Shaw's newer New Women are often simply abundant, independent daugh-ters of the Life Force like Lina, Mrs. George, Margaret Knox and Eliza (after her emancipation). A few of them are something subtler. Starting with Nora in *John Bull,* several of Shaw's heroines constitute a new Shavian type: the girlish type, innocent in a fresh un-Victorian way, refined by civilization yet on fire with God. Barbara, Lavinia, and Jennifer Dubedat are most obviously of this stamp.

If the early possessive heroines culminated in Ann Whitefield, the late girl heroines culminate in Joan. *Saint Joan* is an attempt at sev-eral kinds of synthesis, one of Shaw's periodic attempts to gather to-gether in one work all that had been on his mind through several preceding works, to unite and transcend them. Joan unites the down-to-earth practicality of the Lady Cicely's, the vitality of the Lina's, and carries as far as Shaw can take it the spirituality of the girl heroines. When Mrs. Shaw suggested Joan as a subject to her husband, and when he read the records of Joan's trial as made available by Jules Quicherat, Shaw must have realized that here was an oppor-tunity to study and recreate a person who united in herself so much that he had divided between his practical and his idealistic characters. It almost seems that if Joan had never existed Shaw would have had to invent her.

Harold Fromm

With the crude psychology of heroes and villains proscribed, and
with the new psychology of the unconscious will prescribed, the job
of civilization is to detect unconscious impulses and destroy the obsolete codifications that no longer fit the realities. This, if anything, is
the main activity of Shavian drama—the so-called ripping off the
veils in order to expose the substance underneath. *Sartor Resartus*
would serve as an excellent primer to Shavian philosophy once
Schopenhauer had been digested. But this continual revelation of self
is not mere change—it is development, it is civilization. The later
self is more aware than any of the earlier selves, whether the later self
is a man of fifty looking back at his youth or the twentieth century
looking back at the fifteenth. Both can think more thoughts because
the repertoire of thoughts keeps increasing. "The creative Energy, as
yet neither omnipotent nor omniscient, but ever striving to become
both, proceeds by the method of trial and error, and has still something to live for" (*Pen Portraits*, p. 158). Shaw liked Ibsen's *Emperor
and Galilean* because it told him that "the Kingdom of heaven is
within YOU": For Shaw, Ibsen was saying that *man* is God. Although
he is not yet omniscient or omnipotent, he is constantly arriving closer
to being so, for knowledge truly is power. (The heroes of Shaw's plays
usually know more than the other characters and are consequently
unruffled.)

We can see why Shaw became involved in social problems and in
sociological drama: outworn convention and hollow taboos are hin-
drances to knowledge and are therefore evil. The moral obligation of
the agent of the Life Force is to overthrow these old bonds so that the
latest stage in man's development may express itself and be known.
In the nineteenth century this produced a "movement" which Shaw
called Diabolism. All of the devils were his angels: Ibsen, Nietzsche,
Wagner, and, naturally, Shaw (*Pen Portraits*, pp. 217–20). But since
these moralists lacked respectability (which consists in lauding the established order) they were regarded as immoral, immorality, by Shaw's
definition, being merely the insistence on ideas which are contrary
to those established in society. Shaw relished such utterances as "I am
not an ordinary playwright. . . . I am a specialist in immoral and
heretical plays. My reputation has been gained by my persistent

From Bernard Shaw and the Theatre in the Nineties *by Harold Fromm
(Lawrence, Kansas: University of Kansas Press, 1967, pp. 48–52, 53, 54–55. Copyright
© 1967 by the University of Kansas Press. Reprinted by permission of the publisher.*

struggle to force the public to reconsider its morals" (*Prefaces*, p. 410).
Eric Bentley, using Shaw's own words, has described his plays as
depictions of the "struggle between human vitality and the artificial
system of morality." [1] Shaw's vaunted immorality, and the heretical
doctrines of his plays, are epitomized in statements like this: "The fact
is, armies as we know them are made possible, not by valor in the
rank and file, but by the lack of it; not by physical courage . . . but
by civic impotence and moral cowardice. I am afraid of a soldier, not
because he is a brave man, but because he is so utterly unmanned by
discipline that he will kill me if he is told. . . . I respect a regiment
for a mutiny more than for a hundred victories." [2] Rebellion, far from
being vicious, is the only virtue: "Integrity consists in obeying the
morality which you accept" (I, 176). The conscientious objector, then,
is the hero, not the soldier who fights in the field because he is afraid
of what society will do to him if he refuses. When Golding Bright,
following Shaw's advice, told his father to cut off his allowance, Shaw
wrote: "I congratulate you especially on the fact that all your friends
and relations regard you as a madman. That is an indispensable beginning to a respectable, independent life." [3] "Though we may not all
care to say so, yet it is the rebel against society who interests us; and
we want to see the rebel triumphant rather than crushed or reconciled" (I, 234). The rebel is most likely to be an agent of the Life
Force, because he is most likely to fight for the latest expression of
man's soul against the outworn but accepted expression of a prior
soul. A good portion of *The Sanity of Art* deals with the problem of
the genius who is exempt from conventional morality and legality
and who, instead, makes his own. Most people are content to follow
the established customs, not only for the sake of a quiet life, as Shaw
would say, but for the simple reason that they know no better. Laws
"are made necessary, though we all secretly detest them, by the fact
that the number of people who can think out a line of conduct for
themselves even on one point is very small" (*Essays*, pp. 304–05). Even
a genius accepts more conventions that he is aware of, merely for the
sake of convenience. But on essential issues, in matters of conscience,
the genius will rebel rather than follow the code. And in this way
the Life Force triumphs over the repressive forces of convention: "Law
soon acquires such a good character that people will believe no evil
of it; and at this point it becomes possible for priests and rulers to
commit the most pernicious crimes in the name of law and order.
Creeds and laws come to be regarded as applications to human con-

[1] Eric Bentley, *Bernard Shaw* (Norfolk, Conn., 1957), p. 105.
[2] *Shaw on Theatre*, ed. E. J. West (New York: Hill & Wang, 1958), p. 36. Com-
pare Thoreau's *Civil Disobedience*.
[3] *Advice to a Young Critic*, ed. E. J. West (New York: Crown, 1955), p. 37.

duct of eternal and immutable principles of good and evil; and break-
ers of the law are abhorred as sacrilegious scoundrels to whom nothing
is sacred" (*Essays,* p. 307). Creative evolution, however, moves from
submission and obedience, to willfulness and rebellious self-assertion
(*Essays,* p. 308).

Sylvan Barnet, explaining the relation of this evolution to the role
of comedy, observes that traditional comedy censures deviations from
convention, while Shaw believed that "allegiance to a code is necessarily ludicrous, for it becomes outdated. His comic hero, then, de-
velops, or adopts, a new realistic morality beyond that of his society's
idealism. Shavian comedy is critical not of individuals but of society's
norm, insisting that the individual who pierces illusions is not absurd
but in line with the process of the world spirit." [4] The root of much of
Shaw's criticism of the so-called problem plays of his own day, especially those of Pinero, is to be found in this view of evolution and its
relation to comedy. Much of the material on which supposedly serious
dramatists based their "problems" would actually have been fit for
satiric treatment in comedy.

An interesting sidelight on comedy is Shaw's perception of the shift
in comic materials during the past several hundred years. As the Life
Force refines the mind, subjects that were once treated as hilarious
jokes come to be treated as questions of serious morality. Shaw himself uses *The School for Scandal* to point this out: Sheridan's play is
dated because "Joseph's virtue is a pretence instead of a reality, and
because the women in the play are set apart and regarded as absolutely outside the region of free judgment in which the men act."

*   *   *

For "the function of comedy is to dispel . . . unconsciousness by
turning the searchlight of the keenest moral and intellectual analysis
right on to it" (III, 84). If comedy, then, "is nothing less than the
destruction of old-established morals" (III, 87), it is surely another
agent of the Life Force.

As we see in Shaw's treatment of Shakespeare, not only pure comedy,
but tragicomedy too, is able to deal with the points of view which interest Shaw. He believed that comedy, and especially tragicomedy,
had replaced tragedy as the main force of the drama, chastening behavior through irony, though not through ridicule.[5] Shaw's use of
comedy is explained well by Daniel Bernd: "Shaw is comic, humorous,
and ironic, but not satirical. Shaw is not satirical . . . for the very
simple reason that he did not think it the function of comedy, or

[4] "Bernard Shaw on Tragedy," *PMLA,* LXXI, 892.
[5] *Shaw on Shakespeare,* ed. Edwin Wilson (New York, 1961), pp. 252–54.

any other form of the drama, to administer pain. This is not so surprising when we consider Shaw's ethical position on a broad range of subjects. He objected to punishment, revenge, vivisection, blood sports, killing of animals for food, capital punishment, and any form of cruelty whatever, and more often than not, his objections were based on the evil effects on the perpetrator as much as on the victim." [6]

If geniuses and comedies are chief agents of the Life Force, what are the means whereby an individual can cultivate the Life Force within himself? With will and impulse—not reason—as the mainspring of human life, it is necessary to refine one's emotional and sensuous susceptibilities if one wishes to live at the highest possible level of one's being. This imperative is perfectly in character, coming, as it does, from an esthete, "voluptuary," and puritan.

*   *   *

Shaw tells us in his *Sixteen Self Sketches* that he valued sexual experience mainly because its ecstasy was a foretaste of what normal life would be like after the Life Force had been at work for a very long time. Elsewhere he said that in some dim future men will "experience a sustained ecstasy of thought that will make our sexual ecstasies seem child's play," [7] a subject dealt with in *Back to Methuselah*. Of paramount importance, however, is the fact that feeling precedes thought and that one's feelings must be cultivated before one can have a refined mind. Shaw unconsciously paraphrases another voluptuary-puritan, John Milton (who said that Spenser was a better teacher than Aquinas), when he asks: "Which is the greater education, pray—your tutor, when he coaches you for the Ireland scholarship or Miss Janet Achurch, when she plays Nora for you?" [8] The aim of this refinement of the senses is a phenomenon even higher than thought: mystic ecstasy. Nowhere is this made clearer than in an inspiring flight from "The Religion of the Pianoforte":

> However you may despise romantic novels, however loftily you may be absorbed in the future destiny of what is highest in humanity, so that for mere light literature you turn from Dante to Goethe, or from Schopenhauer to Comte, or from Ruskin to Ibsen—still, if you do not know *Die Zauberflöte,* if you have never soared into the heaven where they sing the choral ending of the Ninth Symphony, if *Der Ring des Nibelungen* is nothing to you but a newspaper phrase, then you are an ignoramus, however eagerly you may pore in your darkened library over

[6] *The Dramatic Theory of George Bernard Shaw,* University of Nebraska Ph.D. Dissertation, 1962, pp. 103–104.

[7] *Shaw on Theatre,* p. 151.

[8] "The Religion of the Pianoforte," *Fortnightly Review,* LV (n.s.), pp. 263–64.

the mere printed labels of those wonders that can only be communicated by the transubstantiation of pure feeling for musical tone [*sic*].[9]

Schopenhauer would not have dissented.

[9] *Ibid.*, pp. 260–61.

Francis Fergusson

The curious convention-of-no-convention of modern realism is often described as that of the fourth wall: we pretend, as audience, that we are not present at all, but behind the invisible fourth wall of the parlor which the stage accurately reproduces. This is a pretense which it is difficult to maintain; and side by side with modern realism many dramatic forms have flourished which frankly accepted the stage as such and the audience as extremely present. Opera, ballet, and many kinds of comedy do so, in modern times, on the plea that they are not quite serious— "only" music, or distraction, or jokes.

Comedy in any period assumes the presence of the audience, and so cannot as such pretend to the strict modern realism of Ibsen and Chekhov. It is certainly true that Chekhov reveals comic aspects of his action and expects the laughter of the audience; but his convention does not admit that relationship between stage and house, and the pretense of unarranged and untheatrical actuality is never broken. Comic genres, on the other hand, accept some sort of limited perspective, shared with the audience, as the basis of the fun; they show human life *as* comic just because they show it as consistent according to some narrowly defined, and hence unreal, basis. They fit Mr. Eliot's definition of a convention: they are agreed-upon distortions, forms or rhythms frankly imposed upon the world of action. When we understand a comic convention we see the play with godlike omniscience; we know what moves the puppets; but we do not take them as real— when Scaramouche gets a beating, we do not feel the blows, but the idea of a beating, at that moment, strikes us as funny. If the beating is too realistic, if it breaks the light rhythms of thought, the fun is gone, and the comedy destroyed. Hence comedy has provided one of the chief clues to the development of unrealistic forms in the modern theater. And hence the purpose, in this inquiry, of considering the Shavian comic inspiration.

From "*The Theatricality of Shaw and Pirandello,*" *in* The Idea of a Theater *by Francis Fergusson (Princeton, N.J.: Princeton University Press, 1949), pp. 178–83. Copyright 1949 by Princeton University Press. Reprinted by permission of Princeton University Press.*

I say "the Shavian inspiration," because Shaw's peculiar comic sense, brilliant, theatrical, and unmistakable as it is, never found a consistent comic convention, comparable to Molière's for instance, in which it could be completely realized. He obviously assumes the audience, he plays to the gallery, from the very beginning; yet in the early part of his career he did not distinguish his aims from the realism of Ibsen. Later he seemed to identify his purposes with Brieux's—in the preface he wrote to Brieux's *Three Plays;* but he never propounds a simple thesis as Brieux, with perfect logic and consistency, always does. In this same preface he pays his respects to the machine-made boulevard entertainment in such scornful terms as would lead one to suppose that he would never use it himself; yet his plays written before the first World War are usually (among other things) sentimental parlor comedies of the boulevard type, "stirred to the tune of perpetual motion" and topped with "the bread sauce of the happy ending," as Henry James describes them. At the same time they have the quality called Shavian, which means something as definite as "quixotic." As Shaw survives from epoch to epoch, however, his thinking and his reading as active as ever, he becomes more and more self-conscious; and though the theater for which he started writing is nearly gone, he himself is brilliantly revealed, sparring upon the bare platform; and so the nature of his comic inspiration comes clear. In this development one may learn something about the peculiar difficulties of modern comedy, and something about the ways in which modern realism is superseded by other and subsequent forms.

Mr. Eric Bentley, in his very useful study *George Bernard Shaw,* has pointed out that Shaw's comedy in its beginnings is based upon the same enlightened drawing room as Oscar Wilde's. *Major Barbara* is an example of this early period in his development. Lady Brit's drawing-room feels as stable and secure as the traditional cosmos of the Greeks or Elizabethans, but it is as clear and small as a photograph; the London version of the bourgeois world. And the story of the play may be read as a typical sentimental parlor comedy for the carriage-trade. Lady Brit is an absurd but likeable pillar of society; her estranged husband, Undershaft, a fabulously wealthy munitions-maker of great wisdom and kindliness; her daughter Barbara a sincere but misguided major in the Salvation Army. She is in love with Cusins, a professor of Greek, a character suggested by Professor Gilbert Murray. The main issues are between Barbara and her father: the relative merits of the Salvation Army and munitions-making as ways to be saved. Cusins disapproves both of the Salvation Army and the Undershaft industry of destruction, but at the end he marries Barbara and places his Greek-trained intellect together with her revivalistic fervor in the service of bigger and better bombs. Shaw apparently wants us to believe in Barbara as a real human being in the round, instead of a caricature, and to take her dramatic conversion to her father's business seriously. At any rate he rejoices, and bids us sentimentally rejoice, at the end of his fable when the girl, the man, and the money are at last brought together. The audience may go home (in spite of the witty dialectics it has heard) in laughter, tears, and complacency, spiced, at most, with a touch of the shocking—for the secure basis of their little world, the eternity of the drawing-room, is never seriously questioned. Where, in all this, is the Shavian quality?

The play may be read as a thesis, a proof that munitions-making is the way to be saved; and this is in fact one of the bases of the many witty debates. It is a wonderfully farcical idea, but Shaw is far from offering it as Brieux offers his theses. As he uses it, it has depths of irony which Brieux never dreamed of: Shaw neither believes nor disbelieves it; its relation to reality is never digested—nor its relation to the sentimental story that Shaw puts with it. Its usefulness lies in its theatrical fertility: it is a paradox which may be endlessly debated, but it is in no sense the truth as Brieux thought he was proving the truth. The characters are conceived on a similar basis of paradox—except Barbara, who, as I have said is supposed to be real. But Lady Brit, Undershaft, and each of the minor characters clearly has his paradoxical platform. Lady Brit's is that she must have both the Undershaft money and the creed of the Church of England. The two are logically incompatible; but granted this non-Euclidean postulate, everything she does follows with unanswerable logic. And so for Undershaft, who presents himself as wise, kind, and completely dedicated to destruction. These platforms no doubt represent clarifications or schematizations of real attitudes in contemporary society. In the play, the rationalized platforms, as they are debated and developed, constitute the brisk mental life which we enjoy; but the relation of this life of the mind—this farce of rationalizing—to the human reality is no more defined than that of the paradoxical thesis to truth. Thus the play is a parlor-game, based upon the freedom of the mind to name and then to rationalize anything, without ever deviating from the concept to the thing—the British Empire and Original Sin as light and portable as the blueprints of the social planners and human engineers. Shaw the moralist invites us into this brisk exchange for therapeutic reasons, as gymnasium-instructors instigate boxing or softball: not to win, not to prove anything, but for the sake of a certain decent fitness in the moral void. But Shaw the clown sees his and our agility as a rather frightening farce.

If one thinks over these elements—the sentimental story, the farcical-profound paradoxical thesis, and the complacency of the audience—one may get spiritual indigestion. But if one sees a performance, one may understand how it all hangs together for those quick two hours: it is because its basis in the upholstered world of the carriage-trade is never violated. On this basis it is acceptable as a string of jokes which touch nothing. And Shavian comedy of this period still flatters and delights our prosperous suburbs. But Shaw himself, as the world changed and the London drawing-room appeared to be less than eternal, became dissatisfied with it. He first began planning *Heartbreak House* about thirty-five years ago.

In *Heartbreak House* the perpetual-motion machine of the dialogue is built on the same basis as in *Major Barbara:* each character has a paradoxical platform to defend, with epithet and logic, in the brisk free-for-all of the emancipated parlor. Hector, for instance, is unanswerable as a vain, erotic housecat and heroic man of action; Captain Shotover as omniscient, morally fit as a fiddle, and a futile old man secretly sustained by rum. The Shavian farcical inspiration is here to be found at its sharpest and deepest. But in this play Shaw comes very close to presenting it with the integrity and objectivity of art: to accepting the limited perspective afforded by his view of action as rationalizing, and to finding the proper dramatic form for its temporal development—neither the boulevard intrigue nor the thesis *à la* Brieux which he had tried to use in *Major Barbara,* but a "fantasia" as he calls it. This notion of dramatic form was derived from Chekhov, as he explains in the preface; and one way to understand the superior consistency and self-consciousness of this play is by comparing it with Chekhov's masterpiece. It was a performance of *The Cherry Orchard* which Shaw saw before the first World War that gave him his clue— precisely because Chekhov saw the prewar drawing room, "cultured, leisured Europe before the war," as Shaw puts it, not as eternal, but as dissolving before our eyes, and the significant mode of human action, not as rationalizing, but as the direct suffering of the perception of change. It was Chekhov's opposite perspective on the bourgeois theater of human life which made Shaw aware of the nature and limitations of his own.

Thus the ostensible scene is still the emancipated parlor; but in *Heartbreak House* this parlor is no longer felt as all reality: we feel around it and behind it the outer darkness, the unmapped forces of the changing modern world. The life of the play is still in the making of epithets and in logical fencing; but now we see that the emancipated mind, though omnipotent in its own realm, is helpless between the power of the wealth and war making business-industrial-financial machine one way, and the trivial or deathly passions of the faithless psyche the other way. And the parlor in which it is free to play its endless game is itself brought into focus as a thin insulating sheath.

Because of this added dimension—because Shaw now places his scene in a wider perspective—he understands the real shape, the temporal development of his action, far more accurately. In this play, as in *The Cherry Orchard,* nothing happens, and nothing is proved or disproved. The people come and go, their love affairs come and go with the pointless facility of the monkey-house; off-stage we are aware of their endless intrigues for money or power. But the interest is centered where it belongs: not on events or narrative sequences, not on what happens to any individual, but on the fateless fate and the bodiless farce of the emancipated mind itself. This, I think is what Shaw means by subtitling the play "A Fantasia in the Russian Manner on English Themes." Chekhov sees his people *as* suffering; Shaw, with his moral fitness, sees them *as* fully awake and sharply rationalizing. That the abstract form of these complementary versions of human action should be so similar is perhaps significant. In any case, the comparison between the two plays offers a good example of what I have called the partial perspectives of the modern theater.

But in spite of its greater artistry and self-consciousness, *Heartbreak House* has its blemishes. Ellie, like Major Barbara, is not quite objectified; the author has, and demands of us, a sympathy for her which violates the convention of farce. And at the end of the play, when the bombs fall and it is time to send the audience home, Shaw cannot resist a little preaching: he seems to wish to say that his farcical vision need not be accepted at all if we will only mend our ways; that we are all right, really. The therapist and drawing-room entertainer is even here not quite replaced by the inspired clown, with his disinterested vision of action as rationalizing in the void. Thus we are brought to the crux of our problem: why is it that the Shavian inspiration, so strong and lively, never quite finds a consistent convention and a completely accepted form?

Shaw never discovered a publicly acceptable, agreed-on basis in reality outside his peculiar comic perspective whereby it might have been consistently and objectively defined. All comedy is conventional and hence unreal; but Shaw does not make the distinction between the real and his own ironic perspective upon it. This is as much as to say that his perspective, or comic inspiration, is that of romantic irony: the basis of his theses, of his rationalized characters, and of the movement of his dialogue is the *unresolved* paradox. If the "emancipated mind" is to be really emancipated, its freedom must be that of the squirrel cage and its life (having neither beginning, middle, nor end) as formless as the squirrel's perpetual race.

In *The Magic Mountain* Hans Castorp and Settembrini are discussing irony. The only variety which Settembrini admits is what he calls "direct, classic irony," in which the ambiguity is a rhetorical device only, and the meaning of the ironist is unmistakable. I should prefer to call it Neoclassic, to distinguish it from Sophoclean irony, and because it is certainly the irony of Molière. For example, consider the platform of Molière's imaginary invalid, Argan: it is absurd as Lady Brit's. Argan is making a career of invalidism and (like a Shavian character) he is prepared to accept all the logical consequences of his position. But in the light of the sturdy common sense of Molière's *honnêtes gens,* to whom the story of Argan is presented, the absurdity and the impossibility are clear from the first. Thus the temporal form of the play is given: it will be a demonstration by *reductio ad absurdum* of Argan's untenable assumptions—i.e., by an appeal from logic to reality, from Argan's rationalizations to what Molière can assume that his audience directly sees. When the demonstration is complete, the play is over; both the comic convention and the dramatic form are objectified with reference to the *common* sense of the audience. It is this common or agreed-on basis which Shaw, like Hans Castorp, will not or cannot have—whether because he cannot rely on a common ground with his audience or because it would limit the freedom of the mind which he demands.

In the beginning of his career (in *Major Barbara,* for instance) the unmanageable depths of the Shavian irony were obscured by the clichés of the parlor comedy which he was ostensibly writing, and by the supposed security of the Edwardian parlor. And Shaw himself hid coyly and more or less successfully behind the pretense of the standard cast of characters. In *Heartbreak House* the parlor has lost its solidity, the rationalized "characters" are more frankly accepted as unreal, and the true Shavian sense of human life as rationalizing in the void almost finds its true form, the "fantasia" or the arbitrarily broken *aria da capo.* Moreover, in *Heartbreak House* we may observe the cognate process: the emergence upon the stage of the ironist himself. It is true that Shaw can be felt in all his plays behind the paper-thin masks of his characters; and it is true that there are representatives of the Shavian *persona* before Captain Shotover. But the Captain, probably Shaw's profoundest farcical figure, is also the most complete representative of Shaw himself. The drawing-room evaporates; the characters evaporate, and the prophet-clown himself appears upon a stage which is now accepted as a real platform before the modern crowd. The basis in reality of romantic irony is in the attitudes of the ironist; and just as everything in *The Magic Mountain* points to the shifting thoughts and feelings of Castorp-Mann, so Shavian comedy is not so much a consistent theatrical form as an extension of the author's own entertaining conceptual play.

Too True to Be Good is not one of Shaw's best plays; indeed he almost abandons the pretense that he is writing a play at all. But at the end, Audrey—the burglar-preacher who obviously represents the author—bursts forth in an impassioned monologue which presents an apocalyptic vision of the nature and destiny of the Shavian theater. As the other characters drift off the stage, bored with Audrey's preaching, he describes them as follows: "There is something fantastic about them, something unreal and perverse, something profoundly unsatisfactory. They are too absurd to be believed in; yet they are not fictions; the newspapers are full of them." He might be describing all of Shaw's characters: unbelievable as people, yet not defined as fictions either; unsatisfactory, now, even to their author. But the ironist's inspiration is unquenched. Alone on the lighted platform before the darkened house, Audrey continues: "And meanwhile my gift has possession of me; I must preach and preach no matter how late the hour and how short the day, no matter whether I have nothing to say." It is the voice of Shaw the genius of farce, at last aware of his real basis. But Shaw the moral therapist (though relegated to the final stage-direction) has still the last word. "But fine words butter no parsnips," he warns us; "the author, though a professional talk-maker, does not believe that the world can be saved by talk alone."

Donald Costello

To Bernard Shaw, the silent cinema was "a much more momentous invention than printing." This extraordinary significance was due not to the artistic value of the motion picture, but to its social force. Shaw the propagandist, the dramatist who insisted that great art can never be anything but intensely and deliberately didactic, had never had any patience with the doctrine of art for art's sake. Art was for the sake of society. And now, with the advent of the cinema, Shaw saw a chance for reforming the whole world through communication. That prospect excited him; the birth of a new art form did not.

The Cinema as a Social Force

The social power of the cinema lay primarily in the fact that it, unlike books, could reach everybody. In a *New Statesman* article of 1914, Shaw explained:

Before printing could affect you, you had to learn to read; and until 1870 you mostly had not learned to read. But even when you had, read-

From "The Fascination of the Serpent's Eye," in The Serpent's Eye: Shaw and the Cinema by Donald Costello (Notre Dame, Ind.: Notre Dame University Press, 1965), pp. 1–4, 83–85. Reprinted by permission of the publisher.

ing was not really a practical business for a manual laborer. Ask any man who has done eight or ten hours' heavy manual labor what happens to him when he takes up a book. He will tell you that he falls asleep in less than two minutes. Now, the cinema tells its story to the illiterate as well as to the literate; and it keeps its victim (if you like to call him so) not only awake but fascinated as if by a serpent's eye. And that is why the cinema is going to produce effects that all the cheap books in the world could never produce.

The effects to be produced by the fascinating serpent's eye of the cinema were monumental. Shaw enumerated some of them: "The cinema is going to form the mind of England. The national conscience, the national ideals and tests of conduct, will be those of the film."

If the mind of England was going to be shaped, Shaw wanted to be in on the shaping. He announced publicly in 1914 that he would be happy to contribute a few sample scenarios to any movie maker who wanted them. This would be the first step, he hoped, in the establishment of a cinematic movement devoted wholly "to the castigation by ridicule of current morality." He was, of course, calling for the establishment of a specifically Shavian cinema, a cinema which, he added, could exist only if the state would endow the cinema so as to place it above the needs of competition. But there were no takers. Shaw the scenarist was not to be born for two decades. In the meantime, to his growing displeasure, Shaw had to limit his attacks on current morality to his plays, his pamphlets, and his speeches. He had to do without the potent social force of the cinema.

Shaw, of course, exploded into wrath at the idea of all that cinematic power being employed for decidedly un-Shavian ends. Indeed, the silent cinema, far from attacking the current conventional morality, was helping to form it and to spread it. The great danger of the cinema was its morality. In his contribution to a symposium on "Education and the Cinematograph" in a 1914 issue of a London journal called *The Bioscope,* Shaw complained that because a film had to go around the world unchallenged if a maximum of profit was to be made from it, the silent cinema was in actuality "not merely ordinarily and locally moral, but extraordinarily and internationally moral." The cinema was the great moral leveller. And, he added, levelling, though excellent in income, is disastrous in morals. Everyone, the London boy and the mining camp denizen, people in cathedral towns and Chinese seaports, everyone was force-fed and fascinated by the same desolating romantic morality. No superman would thus be formed to rise up above the moral level. He was worried that national characteristics and individuals would all be blended: "The next generation of English-men will no longer be English: they will represent a world-average of character and conduct, which means that they will have rather less virtue than is needed to run Lapland." Looking around, Shaw discovered that "the nameless exponents of a world-wide vulgarity (vulgarity is another of the names for morality) have complete possession" of the silent cinema, a cinema without Shaw.

But Shaw's early enthusiasm for the motion picture was not easily crushed. He recognized, even in the silent days when the cinema was under the control of world-wide commercialism and morality, that many indirect advantages kept seeping through the movies. One of the advantages that he admitted was the exposure of the movie-going public to certain principles of beauty: "The cinematograph, by familiarizing us with elegance, grace, beauty, and the rest of those immoral virtues which are so much more important than the moral ones, could easily make our ugliness look ridiculous."

*   *   *

Major Barbara

After the success of *Pygmalion* in the movies, the name of Bernard Shaw was no longer poison to the financiers. Gabriel Pascal found himself holding a financial trump card. Shaw, still glowing with the triumph of *Pygmalion,* expressed the fullest confidence in Pascal, whose producing firm, called General Films, was now allied solidly and publicly with the suddenly valuable Bernard Shaw. Pascal had the advantage not only of Shaw, but of a name almost equally valuable. Cinema critic C. A. Lejeune noted that any film producer in the world "would give his ears" for the new leading lady named Wendy Hiller. Pascal had *her,* too—on contract. The most important factor in the decision to follow *Pygmalion* with *Major Barbara* was Wendy Hiller's desire and availability to play the title role.

With the names of Bernard Shaw and Wendy Hiller waved before them, the financiers came running. Nicholas Davenport and J. Arthur Rank, in on the ground floor, again had a hand in the financing of the film. They were joined by financier C. M. Woolf. And Shaw himself was so enthusiastic about this new film that he even invested in it part of his 10 per cent (before taxes) royalty payment from *Pygmalion*.

The actual filming of *Major Barbara,* in spite of the ease with which Pascal collected the money, never did run smoothly. The war was the major villain. In September of 1940, Pascal cabled to a friend in America: "Everytime we get the camera and players set up and are ready to shoot, we must race for air raid shelters." During one week, air raids allowed only one partial day of filming. Eventually, as the film, originally scheduled for ten weeks' shooting, dragged on into double that time, the players and technicians began ignoring the air raid warnings. Even Shaw, when he was making his trailer which was to appear as his personal introduction to the completed film, refused to go into the shelter during an alarm. By Pascal's own count, Nazi planes dropped 125 bombs in the vicinity of the *Major Barbara* set. The company was often forced to travel more than 100 miles to get out of range of the constant airplane noises. Once, when the company returned to the East End of London to complete a scene which had been started there previously, the houses had disappeared.

War-caused personnel problems also delayed the filming. David Tree, playing Charles Lomax, was called up for duty in the army, but eventually was released so that filming could continue. Andrew Osborn, originally set to play the role of Adolphus Cusins, was drafted, and was replaced by Rex Harrison.

Troubles seemed only to increase the verve of Shaw. The victorious and confident Shaw descended upon General Films and almost cleared out Pascal's studio. He sat down to write *this* screen play himself. Just as Pascal had decided to direct this film without aid, so Shaw decided to write it without aid. In this second Shaw-Pascal film, Shaw alone received screen-play credit: "Scenario and Dialogue by Bernard Shaw." Shaw contributed not only the script for *Major Barbara* but—a bit more than during the filming of *Pygmalion*—his personal presence. Shaw made visits both to the Denham studios and to location filming. While watching the big Salvation Army meeting in Albert Hall, Shaw got so excited that he rushed onto the set, joining the extras in the singing and cheering crowd scene. "My apologies for interfering on Friday," he later wrote to Pascal. In a studio visit on September 12, 1940, Shaw—always interested in the verbal—complained about several language matters, especially the diction of Rex Harrison. Shaw jotted down this note to himself: "Cusins thinks that when an actor is unfortunate enough to have to speak old-fashioned verse, he should be as colloquial as possible so as to make it sound like cup-and-saucer small talk. This of course only throws the verse away. When I write verse it must be deliberately declaimed as such—I mentioned this to Rex."

Chronology of Important Dates

1856	Shaw born in Dublin on July 26.
1879–1883	Five novels: *Immaturity, The Irrational Knot, Love Among the Artists, Cashel Byron's Profession, The Unsocial Socialist*
1882	Heard Henry George, the American Socialist, at a meeting and was moved to read *Das Kapital.*
1884	Became a member of the Fabian Society.
1885–1892	*Widower's Houses.*
1885	Wrote book reviews for *The Pall Mall Gazette.*
1888–1890	Wrote music criticism for *The Star.*
1889	Wrote essays for the Fabian Society.
1891	*The Quintessence of Ibsenism.*
1892	First play, *Widower's Houses,* produced.
1893	*Mrs. Warren's Profession* banned, produced in 1902.
1894	*Arms and The Man* and *Candida.* Shaw skyrockets to fame.
1895–1898	Wrote drama criticism for *The Saturday Review,* later printed as *Our Theatre in the Nineties.*
1895	"The Sanity of Art."
1896	*You Never Can Tell.* "Socialism for Millionaires," later printed as a Fabian tract.
1897	*The Devil's Disciple.*
1898	Married Charlotte Payne-Townshend. *Caesar and Cleopatra* and "The Perfect Wagnente."
1899	*Captain Brassbound's Conversion.*
1901–1903	*Man and Superman,* produced in 1905.

1904–1907	The Vedienne and Granville-Barker Court theatre productions. The association formed when Granville-Barker agreed to do Shakespeare if he could also do Shaw. Shaw became a permanently established theatrical success.
1904	*John Bull's Other Island.*
1905	*Major Barbara.*
1906	*The Doctor's Dilemma.*
1908	*Getting Married.*
1909	*The Shewing-Up of Blanco Posnet.*
1909–1910	*Misalliance.*
1910	*Fanny's First Play*
1911–1912	*Androcles and the Lion.*
1912	*Pygmalion.*
1913–1916	*Heartbreak House.*
1914–1915	"Commonsense About the War."
1921	*Back to Methuselah.*
1923	*Saint Joan.*
1925	Received the Nobel Prize for Literature.
1928	"The Intelligent Woman's Guide to Socialism and Capitalism."
1929	*The Apple Cart.*
1932	*Too True to Be Good.* *The Adventures of the Black Girl in her Search for God.*
1934	*The Simpleton of the Unexpected Isles.*
1936	*The Millionairess.*
1939	*In Good King Charles' Golden Days.*
1947	*Buoyant Billions.*
1950	Died, November 2.

Notes on the Editor and Contributors

ROSE ZIMBARDO, of the State University of New York at Stony Brook, is the author of *Wycherly's Drama* and of articles on Shakespeare (*A Midsummer Night's Dream, The Tempest, Henry V*) as well as modern drama (Genet, Albee, Beckett).

ANTHONY S. ABBOTT, of Davidson College, has studied Elizabethan as well as modern drama. *Shaw and Christianity* is his first book. He has just become bibliographer for *The Shaw Review*.

ERIC BENTLEY, of Columbia University, is the author of several well-known books of criticism on the drama, including *The Playwright as Thinker, In Search of Theatre, The Modern Theatre,* and *The Classic Theatre.*

DONALD COSTELLO, of the University of Notre Dame, is author of *The Generation of the Third Eye,* as well as *The Serpent's Eye.* He is a contributor to scholarly journals and motion picture editor of *Today.*

BERNARD DUKORE, of the City University of New York, has written *Bernard Shaw, Director* and articles on Shaw and other modern dramatists. Mr. Dukore has just become executive director of the Ph.D. program in theater at the City University of New York.

FRANCIS FERGUSSON, of Rutgers University, in addition to his well-known *The Idea of a Theatre* has written two other critical works: *Dante's Drama of the Mind* and *The Human Image in Dramatic Literature.* He has also written a version of Sophocles' *Elektra.*

JOSEPH FRANK, of the University of Rochester, is author of *The Levellers* and *The Beginnings of the English Newspaper,* as well as a study of the minor poetry of the seventeenth century.

HAROLD FROMM, of Brooklyn College of the City University of New York, has written on such various subjects as Spenser's poetry, Emerson, Kierkegaard and historical Christianity, and *To the Lighthouse.* He is interested in music as well as literature.

FRED MAYNE, of The University of Witwatersrand, Johannesburg, South Africa.

MARTIN MEISEL, of Dartmouth University, is completing books on nineteenth-century fiction and drama, and on the work of Carlo Gozzi.

MARGERY MORGAN, of Monash University, Australia, has written several articles on Shaw and Yeats. She is at present completing a book on Shaw, from which the article printed here is an excerpt.

Selected Bibliography

Eric Bentley, *Bernard Shaw*, rev. ed. New York: New Directions, 1957. This book began the revaluation of Shaw and paved the way for objective criticism of the plays themselves. It is an intelligent treatment of the ideas in socialism, economics, and religion that contributed to Shaw's complicated intellectual view.

Henry C. Duffin, *The Quintessence of Bernard Shaw*. London: George Allen and Unwin, 1939. This book is not the definitive critical biography it sets out to be. It is useful, however, for its discussions of ideas in politics, religion, and the relation between the sexes that were the background for Shaw's thinking.

Harold Fromm, *Bernard Shaw and the Theatre of the Nineties*. Boston: Houghton Mifflin, 1967. This excellent book carefully limits the range of its treatment in favor of depth. It is a study of the role Shaw played in relation to English drama during the years he was drama critic for the *Saturday Review*. Since the principles Shaw evolved during this time were his throughout his career, Fromm maintains that drama criticism is the seed of everything Shavian.

Archibald Henderson, *G.B.S.: Man of the Century*. New York: Appleton-Century-Crofts, 1956. This is the standard biography of Shaw. Although it lacks a critical point of view, it is enormously comprehensive. It is useful for the thoroughness with which it presents the events in Shaw's life and, since Henderson was a friend of Shaw's, for Shaw's own comments upon his activities.

William Irvine, *The Universe of George Bernard Shaw*. New York: Whittlesey House, 1949. A critical biography that attempts to illuminate various aspects of Shaw's intellect in relation to the various ideas and systems of thought with which it engaged.

Louis Kronenberger, ed., *George Bernard Shaw: A Critical Survey*. New York: World Publishing Co., 1953. This volume, which contains essays by W. H. Auden, Edmund Wilson, and Alick West, among others, is useful in illustrating the generally low repute in which Shaw was held during the 1930's and 1940's. It also illustrates the degree to which in the criticism

of those years Shaw the man outweighed Shaw the comic artist in importance.

R. J. Kaufmann, ed., *G. B. Shaw: A Collection of Critical Essays.* Englewood
Cliffs, N.J.: Prentice-Hall, 1965. This volume is the Twentieth Century
Views volume on Shaw. It contains excerpts from the best books that have
been done on Shaw.

R. Manden and J. Mitchenson, *Theatrical Companion to Shaw.* London:
Rockliff, 1954. This is a quite useful handbook of theatrical information
about each of Shaw's plays. It provides such information as a short history
of performances, lists of casts, and production arrangements for each of
the plays.

Fred Mayne, *The Wit and Satire of George Bernard Shaw.* New York: St.
Martin's Press, 1967.

Richard Ohmann, *Shaw: The Style and The Man.* Middletown, Conn.:
Wesleyan University Press, 1962. I list these two excellent books together
because the earlier book had to be done in order that the more recent
book be as well conceived and executed as it is. Both are examinations
of Shaw's style. Ohmann's book, the more general treatment, relates Shaw's
style to his particular vision. Mayne's book limits its scope more narrowly,
focusing upon wit and satire as stylistic devices as well as structuring
principles. It also treats subcategories of wit and satire, and comes finally
to give us, by indirection, Shaw's artistic perspective.

Percy J. Smith, *The Unrepentant Pilgrim.* Boston: Houghton Mifflin, 1965.
This is an excellent critical biography of Shaw's formative years. Like
most of the best recent works on Shaw it limits its breadth to achieve
depth. Smith deals with Shaw's youth, his early failure, and his evolution
as a critic, a socialist, and a believer. Although it does not aim at the
inclusiveness of earlier biographies, this book contains a theory about
Shaw's evolution as an artist that gives logical coherence to the events
of his life.